Is It Lust or Legalism?

Discerning the Difference between Sexuality, Sensuality, & Sin

Brad Watson

Copyright © 2002 by Brad Watson

Is It Lust or Legalism?
by Brad Watson

Printed in the United States of America

Library of Congress Control Number: 2002108846
ISBN 1-591601-51-7

All rights reserved. No part of this publication may be reproduced or transmitted in any form or by any means without written permission of the publisher.

Unless otherwise identified, Scripture quotations in this book are from the *HOLY BIBLE, NEW INTERNA-TIONAL VERSION, NIV*, copyright 1973, 1978, and 1984, by International Bible Society. Used by permission of Zondervan Publishing House. All rights reserved.

Excerpts from *Sex for Christians* by Lewis Smedes, copyright 1976, 1994, are used by permission from the publisher, Wm. B. Eerdmans Publishing.

Excerpts from "Sexuality and Singleness," *Readings in Christian Ethics* by Richard J. Foster, copyright 1996, are used by permission of the publisher, Baker Books.

Excerpts from The New American Commentary, Volume 22, by Craig Blomberg, copyright 1992, are used by permission of the publisher, Broadman and Holman.

Excerpts from Adultery: An Exploration of Love and Marriage by Robert and Mollie Brow, (www.brow.on.ca./ Books/Adultery) are used by permission of the authors.

Xulon Press
11350 Random Hills Road
Suite 800
Fairfax, VA 22030
(703) 279-6511
XulonPress.com

To order additional copies, call 1-866-909-BOOK (2665).

Dedication

This book is dedicated to my precious wife, Sheila.
Thanks for being my lover, confidant, biggest supporter,
very best friend, faithful companion, and spiritual partner
on this wonderful journey of life. I love you dearly!
Thanks for believing…

Contents

Introduction

R-movies, PG-13 movies, album covers, cable TV, Baywatch, Victoria Secret, Hooters, Maxim, Stuff, Vanity Fair, Rolling Stones, Cosmopolitan, GQ, beaches, lakes, gymnasiums...etc...etc...etc.

The list goes on and on: magazines, movies, and models; beaches, bikinis, and billboards. The world is full of sexual stimuli. There is no escape.

As Christians we hope for eternity but live in the present. We worship on Sundays, but walk on Mondays through a world filled with contradictions: Exciting changes; prophetic promise; growing enlightenment and moral decay—all at the same time competing for our attention.

We talk about holiness, but many of us feel it's like "pie in the sky," an impossible dream. As people of God we think about eternal truths, but realize we still live in the flesh. We yawn, yell, grow tired and sleep. We feel, need, yearn, and experience. We're happy, angry, sad, sexy, and sorry – truly God's sons and daughters and yet fully human at the same time.

There's got to be a way; a way to live at peace with our humanity and yet soar in our spirits.

Is it possible to be sensual and spiritual at the same time? I, for one, believe the answer is yes. Can one be stimulated by food, sex, music, writings, nature, people and feelings and yet still be completely controlled by the Spirit of God? Again, I believe the answer is yes.

Is my sexuality a curse to be endured? I believe the answer is no. Am I displeasing to God if I continue to find people other than my Christian spouse sexually appealing? Again, I think the answer is no. Is it ok to be sexually alive and single at the same time? Is masturbation necessarily a "cop-out"....?

God is not afraid of our sensuality. He made us that way, on purpose. Neither is he embarrassed by these questions, or by the fact that I'm addressing them in this book.

I believe it is time for Christians to get a better worldview: A new paradigm that has God in the center, but all of life (including sexuality and pleasure) circling that center in beautiful orbit. There is no reason why regular people have to go around feeling "dirty" and disconnected to God because of their humanity.

A new concept of "revival" is being birthed in this strategic hour. No longer are revival experiences limited to encounters with God behind the safety of church walls, protected from the sensuality and fleshiness of the world. Now God is touching real people in real life with real anointing from Heaven.

God has become FLESH and dwelt among us. (John 1:14) We are experiencing a renewal of *incarnation* – the presence of a Holy God dwelling in a stable full of animals and manure. A God that is not easily offended; a God who cares about the weaknesses and vulnerabilities of His creatures, but dwells with them anyway!

This, our Father in Heaven has waited for: A time when spirituality and sensuality could meet together in holy embrace; a moment when pure religion would break down the barriers of artificial separation and destroy walls that divide.

God has been waiting for His body to begin to look like

Jesus: A Jesus that can be touched, enjoyed, and appreciated by normal people in the world; a Jesus who enjoys laughter, good food and good company; a Jesus who turns water into wine and mourning into gladness.

Yes, it's time for a new incarnation of a loving God who desires to make Himself known through what He has created. For everything He has created is good, and His children will learn how to "redeem" all things for His glorious, loving, Kingdom purposes.

Please read this book with a prayerful heart. Embrace fully the freedom that your Christian walk brings. At the same time, ask God's loving Spirit to take total control of your life so that your freedom will produce good fruit instead of bad.

Mature Christians should feel completely justified but dissatisfied with themselves at the same time! How can that be? Completely justified, because we know that He has freed us from our sins; always dissatisfied, because we are convinced there is still more of God's power, presence, and purpose to apprehend.

May God deliver you from religious rule-keeping and bring you into the glorious freedom of His Sons and Daughters. May you become more happy, relevant, and real. At the same time, may you become more intensely committed, faithful, and powerful in God.

May you not be intimidated any more by the world; instead, may your light burn even more brightly as your life proclaims to the world the glory of God!

"Instead of their shame my people will receive a double portion, and instead of disgrace, they will rejoice in their inheritance; and so they will inherit a double portion in their land, and everlasting joy will be theirs...Their descendants will be known among the nations...All who see them will acknowledge that they are a people the Lord has blessed." (Isaiah 61:7, 9)

CHAPTER I

Sex and the Sanctuary

It's a cold dark night in a cave far from any other person. The 3rd century monk has left the world of people to go on a solitary religious quest. His desire is two-fold: To know God on the one hand, and to abolish the power of the flesh on the other. His prayers are desperate, his passion is real, but he is still failing. Instead of gaining the victory over his flesh this dark night, he feels tormented more than ever before by the "beast" of his own sexual desire. For to the monk in the cave, victory is not really complete until there are no more sexual thoughts or desires lurking about in his mind. It is simply not good enough just to live a life of celibacy, but the man of God must gain complete victory over his thoughts as well. No sexual desires, fantasies, or images would be allowed to pollute the canvas of his otherwise holy mind. But oh, how this complete breakthrough was rare, even in the testimonies of the godliest and most respected of monks.

Not only were sexual fantasies considered wrong, but even nocturnal emissions of semen were seen as evidence of the continuing control of the flesh (sinful nature) and work of the enemy. Young monks were counseled not to think about women before they went to bed, and even avoided reading Holy books which mentioned the opposite sex.

To get the ultimate victory these ancient saints tried everything! Ammonius burned his body with an iron whenever he had an impure thought; Pachon held an asp against his genital organs; Evagrius spent many nights in a frozen well.[1] Benedict threw himself naked into thick briars and nettles which tore his flesh thinking that the wounds on his body would cure the lust-wound in his soul.[2]

One monk agreed one night to take a woman into his cave who was lost in the desert. To keep from temptation he burned his fingers on his lamp all night long to remind himself of the eternal punishment awaiting those who fell. Another monk who had often thought about the beauty of a woman he once met, when hearing that she had died, went and put his coat on her decomposed body so that the smell of dead flesh would help him fight his constant thoughts of her beauty.[3] Three famous monastic codes penalized the men of God by demanding that any monk found speaking alone with a woman be whipped between 100-200 times because of the supposed compromise.[4] Even Origin, the famous fourth-century Christian leader, castrated himself in an attempt to become sexually pure and be completely free of sexual temptation. Similarly, Jerome said, "Blessed is the man who dashes his genitals against the stone."[5]

Yes, the early church was obsessed with sex! They were obsessed with getting rid of its continual presence and power. They felt that sexual desire was a result of the fall, an evil distraction keeping them from their high spiritual calling. Unfortunately, many times their efforts to abolish all sexual desire simply exasturbated the problem. Some desert monks actually gained a bad reputation for running into the villages and having sex with young women or even boys because they just couldn't fight "the beast" any longer! Their enormous fixation on fighting lust actually had the opposite affect and strengthened its power instead. As sociologist Geoffrey May expressed:

> *"In attempting to desexualize the idea of man, ascetic Christianity succeeded only in over-sexualizing the idea of woman."* [6]

Even the godliest of monks admitted a continual struggle, battle and frustration with sexual desire.

Though they were Christians, this "holy mission" by many in the early church to eradicate sexual desire was actually more influenced by pagan religions and philosophies than it was by Scriptures or by the Spirit of God. Early pagan religions had on the one hand sexual license, on the other sexual asceticism (rigid self-denial). Many important philosophers of the time followed the famous world-renowned pagan thinker, Plato, and lamented the fact that otherwise enlightened people had to put up with "dirty" flesh. In his famous work, *Phaido,* Plato said:

> *It seems that so long as we are alive, we shall continue closest to knowledge if we avoid as much as we can all contact and association with the body, except when they are absolutely necessary; and instead of allowing ourselves to become infected with its nature, purify ourselves from it until God himself gives us deliverance."* [7]

For many ancient philosophers like Plato, life was a continual war between "matter" and "spirit." Everything "fleshy" or "sensual" was material and thus a hindrance to discovering spiritual enlightenment or finding truth.

The Apostle Paul was familiar with the vocabulary and teachings of these moral philosophers of his time, but did not agree with their view of life. Paul had no problem with the body, pleasure, or human sexuality. His own celibacy He saw as a "gift from God" (1 Corinthians 7:6-7) for his specific life and call. He did not believe celibacy should be the goal of every devout Christian, nor did he teach against sensual pleasure. He did teach against the "flesh." The Greek word he used, "*sarx,*" translated "flesh" in the King James Version of Scripture, is called the "sinful nature" by more contemporary versions of the Bible. Discussions of the "flesh" were common in Greek philosophical circles, so Paul made use of this common terminology. His teaching on the flesh, however, was far removed from what Plato or other Greek philosophers had taught.

To the Apostle Paul, the flesh is the *sinful nature* that exists because of man's "fall." (Romans 5) This sinful nature creates a continual struggle or battle within the heart and soul of moral people. For Paul, even when people come to Christ, the sinful nature remains a continuing force to be reckoned with, tempting believers to act selfishly or godlessly. To the Romans Paul said:

> *I know that nothing good lives in me, that is, in my sinful nature. For I have the desire to do what is good, but I cannot carry it out. For what I do is not the good I want to do; no, the evil I do not want to do – this I keep on doing. Now if I do what I do not want to do, it is no longer I who do it, but it is sin living inside me that does it. So I find this law at work: When I want to do good, evil is right there with me. (Romans 7: 18-21)*

After acknowledging humanity's common struggle, Paul rejoices that the solution to the problem has been given to Christians through the Holy Spirit who indwells them. Though the Spirit does not completely eradicate the sinful nature, it does give the Spirit-empowered believer authority over it. (Romans 8) The sinful nature, according to Paul, is an "evil" within – a "sin living inside me." It is not simply the desire for good food, good sex, or pleasure, but it is an *evil bent* towards selfishness. It's a coveting for personal gain at the expense of another and an idolizing of personal agenda rather than a submission to the will of God.

For Paul, therefore, people that live enslaved to the sinful nature or flesh are not those who enjoy the pleasures of life, but people who live selfishly, in opposition to perfect love. Love for God and love for one for another was the foundation of Jesus' teaching. Based on that foundation Paul taught that walking in the flesh was living selfishly, doing the unloving thing rather than representing Christ accurately to others. Consider his instructive words to the Galatians:

> *"You, my brothers, were called to be free. But do not use your freedom to indulge the sinful nature (flesh); rather, serve one another in love. The entire law is summed up in a single command: Love your neighbor as yourself...So I say, live by the Spirit, and you will not gratify the desires of the sinful nature." (Galatians 5: 13-14, 16)*

In the years after the Apostle Paul wrote the letters recorded in the New Testament, many Greco-Roman Christian leaders merged his teaching about the "flesh" with the prevailing Greek ascetic philosophies and came up with a toxic mix! Instead of identifying the flesh as the selfish center, they begin to interpret it as the body and all sensual desire. Because of this, many began to believe that everything associated with the material world and the senses should be looked upon suspectly. Adding to this poisonous mix were works-based religious influences coming from pagan sources that threatened to turn Christianity from a relationship-based and Spirit-led walk into a works oriented, sin-conscious religion.

Although the church never lost its foundational under-standing of grace, it began to struggle, and has continued to struggle for almost two millennia to rid itself of anti-body, anti-pleasure, bad theology. As a result, Christian people have had a difficult time understanding and properly relating to their sexuality. For centuries even marital sexual desire was seen as suspect. The famous theologian, St. Augustine, was greatly influenced by Plato and believed that sex, though necessary, was largely an evil endeavor. He said:

> *"... nothing so cast down the manly mind from its height as the fondling of women and those bodily contacts which belong to the married state."*[9]

According to St. Augustine, only when procreation (the birthing of babies) was the goal was sex permissible. And if husbands and wives had too much fun and pleasure in their sexual intimacy, they were guilty of lust![9] Augustine's defi-nition of lust was obviously far different than what the writ-ers of Scripture implied when they used the term.

For the Biblical writers, lust simply meant "to covet." Later on in this book I will suggest an expanded definition as we examine the different contexts in which the word is used (both positively and negatively) in Scripture. For Augustine, however, lust simply meant sexual drive and desire. In his understanding, this was ALWAYS wrong. He believed that passion was only added to human sexuality as a result of man's fall from grace. In the Garden of Eden, then, there was only passionless, self-controlled sex before the fall. "Away the thought," he exclaims, "that there should have been any unregulated excitement, or the need to resist desire." [10]

Though greatly used of God in other areas, Augustine's hang-ups hindered the church from moving into a more mature understanding of human sexuality. Unfortunately, the influence of his bad sexual theology has remained. Many Christians today still have accepted his faulty definition of lust and therefore condemned themselves to a lifetime of apparent failure. Many modern Catholics still believe that too much passion in marital sex is sinful. Protestants usually do not see marital sex as a problem, but continue to view any sexual stimulation, awareness, or arousal outside of marriage as lust. Not only are these perspectives unbiblical, but they put undue weights of guilt around peoples' necks.

Until recently even discussions about sexual passion were forbidden in many Christian circles. In the early 80's , Dr. James Dobson of Focus on the Family fame broke new ground when he talked publicly about marital sex in a film series which made the rounds in many conservative, evangelical churches. The words "penis" and "clitoris" had never been uttered in many churches up until that time.

Sadly, not only was discussion about sexuality off limits in many churches, but in many Christian marriages as well. Sex language was often seen as "vulgar" or "dirty." Because of the taboo, many couples, even after they married, never clearly communicated to one another about their sexuality. Dr. Dobson spoke of one tragic situation where a couple had been married a number of years but had no success experiencing sexual orgasms. In a private interview, Dr. Dobson realized the man knew nothing about the female clitoris and had never discovered how to make intercourse pleasurable for his wife. After a few minutes of simple instruction, the man was sent home to change his marriage. This story ends successfully with a completely transformed sex life for the deprived couple, but unfortunately, many sad situations do not share this happy ending. Heartbreaking tales can still be told by thousands of Christians all over the world who have never experienced sexual wholeness.

Some say that the "sexual revolution" of the 1970's (and

beyond) was a moral disaster. Certainly the devil had his way with many. But I believe that God also had a holy agenda that was running parallel to the enemy's antics. The Lord was working to change old stereotypes and bring new freedom, dignity, and opportunity to women. At the same time He was (and still is) calling forth fatherhood in men and destroying the old macho mindsets that kept many men from being sensitive, nurturing, and supportive of their wives and families. And in the bedroom, there has been an awakening of intimacy, an increase of passion, and a maturing of the erotic. Sex is moving away from mere animal magnetism and biological release into real communication and shared pleasure for many couples. Sex is not evil, but good. It should not be seen as the devil's toy or the church's headache, but a God-given gift to bring joy, pleasure, intimacy, and new life.

CHAPTER 2

Sexual Sanity for the Soul

The pastor was confused. He had recently come through a wonderful transition in his life and ministry into a freer, less legalistic expression of Christianity. Aligned with a group of likeminded pastors and churches, he felt connected to these older brothers in the Lord and asked them one day for some counsel. "I am blessed by sacred dance in worship," he said, "but I have a struggle: When I see the woman who leads the dance moving so beautifully and gracefully, I have a problem. Though my heart is lifted up in worship, I find myself struggling with her beauty." The other pastors nodded in polite affirmation, but soon changed the subject.

The man's so-called struggle was not really a struggle between purity and lust, but between freedom and legalism. This dear pastor, a personal friend of mine, has a wonderful, strong marriage. He never had any intention of leaving his wife and running off with the dance leader in question. Actually, he wasn't really wrestling with sexual temptation, but with church tradition. My pastor friend was simply taken by the woman's beauty and femininity. The fact of the matter is that the church is still not comfortable with basic God-given human beauty and sexuality. By sexuality, I don't mean intercourse, but our sexual awareness as men and women; our recognition of the desirability of one another, and our appreciation for the things in one another that we find attractive and "worthy of praise." Though the outright, outrageous teaching of the early church against sexuality is no longer with us, there remains under the surface a lingering uncomfortable confusion about what is and what is not appropriate to think, say, feel, or act upon when our God-given human sexuality or sensuality is a factor.

Though it's not quite as obvious, the anti-body, anti-sex, anti-pleasure theology which plagued the church for 1700 years still permeates much of modern Christian thought. Though God certainly wants His people accountable for their sexuality, the enemy has used this vital part of our humanity to torment us with confusion, accusation, condemnation, and guilt. Because of uncertainty in knowing how to accept ourselves and relate to others as sexually alive people, we often find ourselves defenseless to the onslaught of the enemy. The reason some believers are falling into sexual sin is because they have never fully understood how to function maturely as sexually alive and sexually aware Christians.

Many devoted believers love God dearly but have never made real peace with their own sexual desires. They want to please God but need some kind of sexual release. Unfortunately, many of these folks have fallen into sin feeling "trapped" by sexual desires with no place to go. Having tried in vain to run away from all sources of temptation, they have discovered to their dismay that there really is no place to run and hide. Sex follows them, because sex is part of who they are.

"Oh, but I've overcome my sexual passion," some inspired Christian leader tells the men in his church. Interestingly, however, some people's "victory" over sexual stimulation is simply a result of decreased testosterone in their body. Testosterone is one of the hormonal "building blocks" of human growth and sexuality. Doctors have known for many years that testosterone is responsible for "libido" or sexual drive in both men and women. As men grow older, testosterone levels often decrease significantly. Recent studies have indicated that the "testosterone falloff" often begins with men in their 30's, and even temporarily decreases when men become fathers.[11] This is not to say that all sexual desire vanishes, but it certainly can decrease.

On the other hand, some men have an unusually high level of the hormone in their blood. These guys will usually have a much higher sexual drive than the men with lower testosterone levels. Does this mean that lower testosterone is a holier state of being? Or do young people have to live with defeat simply because their testosterone levels are so high?

Perhaps God never intended testosterone to be a curse, but a blessing! But how can the fuel that fires our sexual desire be a blessing? Maybe we need to rethink sexual desire in the first place. Perhaps sexual attraction and desire are not as evil as some have thought.

Many Christians have a serious misunderstanding about their sexual drive. They tend to interpret much of their normal sexual awareness and responsiveness as lust. Much of what has been referred to as "lust" is simply an awareness of sexual attraction or an appreciation for sexual beauty. But many believers feel distant from God when they consider their innermost sexual thoughts and desires. Certainly a Holy God cannot be happy with such low, base feelings. We forget, however, that the God who created the power of sexual attraction is not offended by its presence.

Throughout the history of the church some people have acted as if holiness is authenticated by lack of sexual interest. But as we have seen, it may simply be that some people have a lower sex drive than others. Sexual desire or libido can be measured to some degree by the levels of God-given hormones in our bloodstream. We shouldn't "over spiritualize" everything. We are not just dealing with spiritual, but biological issues as well.

In a similar way, some have criticized all overweight people, assuming that their obesity is always a result of an undisciplined lifestyle or irresponsible eating habits. Recent medical research has shown that some obese people eat exactly the same foods as skinny people and yet remain overweight. The issue is not always discipline, but sometimes metabolism instead. A person with a slow metabolic rate will often put on more weight than someone else who has a high metabolism. Many of us have been frustrated watching skinny people put away junk-food, seemingly eating whatever they want and yet not putting on a single pound! Is it right for the slender person with a high metabolism to claim spiritual superiority because he or she does not carry as much extra weight? Of course not! But isn't it just as ridiculous and wrong for people with lower testosterone levels to claim greater spiritual maturity over others simply because they may not think about sex as much or respond to sexual stimuli in the same way as those with higher testosterone levels and a more potent sex drive? In fact, they may not be more spiritually mature at all! It may have nothing at all to do with spirituality and everything to do with body chemistry. In such cases, these people's lack of sexual interest probably is more of a biological than spiritual phenomena.

If, as Augustine maintained, sexual desire equals lust, then Christians have a real problem. On the other hand, if lust is something altogether different than desire, then perhaps we are alright. Maybe it's not God, but Satan "disguised as an angel of light" (2 Corinthians 11:14) who is telling God's people that something is wrong with them if they experience sexual attraction and desire.

It's my hope that this book will be used of God to eliminate some of the fear and false guilt associated with our human sexuality. I am confident that God desires to give us total victory and clarity about this controversial issue. He has promised to personally instruct us by His Holy Spirit:

> *"As for you, the anointing you received from him remains in you...as his anointing teaches you about all things and as that anointing is real, not counterfeit –just as it has taught you, remain in him." (1 John 2:27)*

God has truly given us everything we need to walk in complete victory. He will certainly teach us about "all things," and that includes our sexuality. He also promises to lead us victoriously by the presence and power of His Spirit. To walk in this freedom, it is critical that we rid ourselves of any "religious spirit" or tradition of men that makes us feel unnecessarily guilty about normal sexual responsiveness. God is for us, not against us, and through a fresh look at Scripture, many chains of tradition will be broken, and many conscientious Christians set free!

Sexual sin is real. Christians must be responsible with their sexuality or it can destroy them. But another problem exists for believers. And in many ways it is just as deadly as sin. It's a problem with "false guilt' which is often stirred up by accusations that come from the enemy's camp. Although sexual sin is definitely a great hindrance to the work of God, so is this illegitimate accusation of the enemy. As in the days of Jesus' earthly ministry, there are still "Pharisee spirits" running around putting burdens on people that are too difficult for them to bear. Speaking of the Pharisees, Jesus said:

> *"They tie up heavy loads and put them on men's shoulders, but they themselves are not willing to*

lift a finger to move them." (Matthew 23:4)

I say "Pharisee spirits" because it is not just legalistic human teachers, but also actual evil spirits throwing accusing thoughts into the arena of our minds to make us feel unworthy.

After feeling "flush" or after being stimulated in some way by someone other than their spouse, many Christians feel ashamed and believe they have sinned. But in most cases, no sin has actually been committed. It's just the enemy, who "prowls around like a roaring lion looking for someone to devour," (1 Peter 5:8) accusing God's people and exploiting their human vulnerabilities. (Revelation 12:10) The guiltier the devil makes us feel, the less likely we will be to reflect the glory of God. As long as the enemy can get us to focus on failure, temptation, or even perceived weakness, we will not be aggressively building ourselves up with the promises of God.

Accusation is a demonic assault and is one of the most subtle and deadly schemes our enemy uses to get us off track. For those who listen to the lies, a mindset (or stronghold – 2 Corinthians 10) is established that fosters a works-righteousness mentality and undermines the grace of God. And in the few and far between moments when we actually feel clean, this mindset continues to destroy grace by promoting an ugly self-righteousness. If left unchecked, the believer under this influence will continually find fault with himself/herself and everyone else as well. Like a rare disease, this mental malady often goes undetected or is misdiagnosed. Because of the false accusations, some precious souls become convinced that to really become holy, they must fight off all sexual sensations and eradicate all earthly desires.

The sad reality of this struggle, however, is that those who think this way are fighting a losing battle! God rarely grants people's pleas to be freed from all sexual drives and earthly, human desires. No matter how intensely these prayers are prayed, they go against God's primary purpose in making us as humans connected to this planet (Even our very makeup is of the soil of the ground, Genesis 2:7). Though He usually won't grant our requests to escape, He will, however, give us grace to live victoriously while we remain in this human body. We are not called to be non-humans, but redeemed humans! The Lord is not pulling us out of the world just yet, but making us its' light instead.

So attempts to eliminate all extra-marital sexual stimuli and desire will usually not work. Although such attempts may seem successful for a season, they will usually ultimately fail. Some of you in trying to accomplish this may have experienced periodic spiritual highs in intense worship times or at conferences, but often later found yourself discouraged and feeling defeated. In spite of what you may have been feeling, God did not abandon you, nor has he been unfaithful. For it was never His divine purpose to do away with your sexual desire in the first place! It's really ok for Christians to be sexually sensitive and even sexually stimulated. Our Heavenly father created us that way! Sexual desire is not in evil in itself. The key is what you do with it.

Please don't misunderstand me! Obviously there are those who do truly have a problem with illegitimate sinful lust and just need to stop living destructive lifestyles. There are men and women of all ages and backgrounds who struggle as sex addicts and are in bondage to sexual sin. Those who fight this difficult battle need help and can be set free!

It is interesting, however, that a psychologist who works with sexually obsessed people recently revealed that a large percentage of his patients come from very religious, sexually restrictive backgrounds. It seems that the rigid, monk-like approach to ridding oneself of sexual desires can actually create the opposite effect.

One simply needs to read the newspapers or watch the

evening news to hear about all the cases of Roman Catholic priests who are being charged with sexual deviance. One researcher said that the list of priests who have sexually abused their parishioners may be 1500 or more in the US alone![12] It is not that Catholics are less spiritual than the Protestants (there have, of course, been many sex scandals in conservative, Protestant circles as well); but it is interesting that the very men who are "swearing away" their sexuality are some of the ones struggling the most with it. Prohibition often has the effect of increasing the very thing it is trying to stop!

God has a better way; a path full of grace, freedom, and self-control. Moderation and self-control are usually more beneficial in the long run in dealing maturely and realistically with earthly, temporal desires than simply trying to turn those desires "off" and hope they've gone away.

Today, for better or worse, we live in a sexually charged atmosphere. Any normal, alert, and alive person will be exposed on a daily basis to various sexual stimuli. While some have unsuccessfully attempted to turn off their sexuality, other Christians have just tried the old "run and hide" strategy. "If I can just *avoid* sexual stimulation and temptation," someone suggests, "then I can overcome." But that is becoming increasingly difficult.

Except at a Christian retreat, (and many times, not even there), few places exist in the world today where one can truly escape. One recent article in a Christian Men's magazine revealed much of the current thinking in many conservative churches regarding strategies to "fight lust." The author bemoaned the fact that a *"Hooters"* restaurant (known for hiring buxom women who wait tables in short-shorts) had recently opened in his town. He suggested that for him to remain holy and lust-free, he had to change the route by which he returned home after work. Not to criticize the man for trying to live by his conscience, but how realistic is a continual avoidance strategy in getting real victory against lust? And for that matter, what constitutes sinful lust anyway? Is it lustful and wrong to experience any kind of sexual desire or draw?

In similar article, another writer suggested that men should wear a rubber band on their wrists and snap it every time they experienced a lustful thought. Sounds a little bit like the desert monks we looked at earlier! Is this author implying that every time anyone becomes sexually stimulated it equals sinful lust and should be punished by pain?

While the "run and hide" strategy may occasionally help some, it cannot be the permanent solution to living lust free. As a pastor and overseer of a number of churches, I have the great privilege of traveling to other nations and cultures. In some of these cultures seeing topless women either on signs or in person is a daily occurrence. How does someone in that cultural setting successfully practice the avoidance strategy? Should Christians in these settings just abandon the culture altogether and live completely to themselves?

There has got to be a better way and a healthier understanding of human sexuality within the Kingdom of God. God has not called us to run away from the world, but to impact it with the love of God. We are not called to be escape artists, but torches, shining the light of God's Kingdom into dark places. It must, then, be possible to live victoriously without simply running away!

How then do we understand our sexual selves and relate to one another as gender-defined and gender-sensitive sexual beings? Can we distinguish between innocent sensuality, sexuality and sinful lust? Again, an extremely important question is what really constitutes sinful lust in the first place?

These critical questions beg for biblically sound and Spirit-led answers. And there are more: Do I need to resign myself to living with a constant internal battle raging every minute against lust? Will I have to keep a collection of rubber bands (or worse) in my closet to inflict pain whenever I am aroused? Is it necessary to change my driving routes to insure that I am not "polluted" by sexual signs or businesses along the way?

These issues are not the nagging questions of the few, but the unspoken struggles of the masses. May God open our hearts to His truth and perspective as we study these issues, and may He give us wisdom and understanding to know what it means to be sexual people living victoriously in a sexually-charged world.

CHAPTER 3

The Heart of the Matter

My Struggle

I can still see the shag green carpet under my prostrate body and bowed head. I was a young man with raging hormones – passionate for God but developing sexually as well. In an agonizing moment, I wanted to scream out with frustration as I fruitlessly attempted to shut out of my mind sexual images that kept interrupting a holy moment of prayer. Like Paul my cry was: "who will rescue me from this wretched body of death." (Romans 7:24) I felt dirty, defeated, and distant from God. This frustrating internal civil war continued for quite some time. Finally, after months of struggle, a light of truth illuminated the darkness of my despair. These tormenting thoughts were in my HEAD, yes, but certainly not in my HEART. I knew I had no intention of acting out these fantasies in any way. They were not really me. They were not my goal or my ultimate desire – being faithful and obedient to God was my real passion. A sense of relief swept over me as I finally learned to simply ignore these mental images. Not to dwell on them, repent for them, or give them undue attention; but simply ignoring them was the strategy that seemed to come from above. And as I learned to laugh at the ridiculous images and leave them alone, they suddenly begin to disappear! Joy returned to my heart, and my prayer life became rich and intense. I learned a great lesson through this struggle - not every thought in my mind had to make its way into my heart. I was not the summation of all my thoughts. The "real me" was deeper and more mature than the traffic jam of thoughts and ideas that went through my head.

The motive of the heart

One of the most common mistakes in defining lust is to attribute to the heart everything that goes on in the mind. Though the heart and mind are related, they are not one in the same. Biblically speaking, thoughts in the mind and the intentions of the heart must be differentiated. Not every thought of the mind corresponds to a decision of the heart. In Scripture, James reminds us that even demons acknowledge Christ in their heads, but have no commitment of heart to his rule and reign (James 2:19) . Jesus Himself said many would have a form of religiosity in their lives; even calling Him 'Lord' with their lips, but their hearts would be far from Him. (Matthew 7:21-23)

Bible believing Christians preach passionately to individuals who have already pledged "mental assent" to the existence of God, but have never given Him their hearts. Many people live in this realm of cognitive or mental acknowledgment of God, but have never had a real conversion experience- a transformation of life that springs out of a heart encounter with God. (Acts 2:37) It is clear then that genuine faith must impact the heart of man, not simply the mind, to change one's life and establish real relationship with God.

It's interesting to observe that although we understand this separation of the mind and heart in matters of salvation, we do not often consider it when we think of temptation and sin. Many people mistake innocent attraction or desire for sinful lust. Even desire that tempts someone to do wrong is not actual sin until that temptation is acted upon. According to James, desire has to "conceive" before "it gives birth to sin." (James 1:14-15). For desire to reach this point of "conception," one must first be "dragged away" and "enticed," according to this Scripture. Simply noticing a beautiful woman or handsome man and admiring their beauty is not the same thing as being "dragged away" or enticed. It's when temptation actually leads to *tasting* forbidden fruit that sin is born.

A decision in the heart must be made to pursue forbidden pleasure before desire actually becomes real sin. Desire in itself is not wrong. The mind and the heart are interconnected and yet separated in Biblical theology. What makes a person holy or unholy will be determined not by what is going on in the mind, but by what is believed or prioritized in the heart.

This internal "line" within the soul separating the mind from the heart is important to discern when talking about the rightness or wrongness of sexual desire. Sexual desire is God-given. It is not something to be ashamed of or a demon to be "cast out." Sexual desire only becomes evil when it becomes obsessive (and therefore idolatrous), or when one begins "acting out" inappropriately in relationship to others. Desires and even temptations in the mind are not a spiritual problem unless they become lodged in the heart and acted out in real-life scenarios.

Adultery of the Heart

In the Sermon on the Mount, Jesus did not condemn physical attraction or sexual desire but "adultery of the heart." (Matthew 5:28). Only when lust infiltrates and begins to negatively influence the heart does it have a corrupting effect upon the Christian life. Only then can it truly be called "sinful lust."

Several years ago, Fuller Seminary professor Lewis Smedes shook up the Christian world when he came out with his groundbreaking book, **Sex and Christians**. In this work, Dr. Smedes challenged Christians to differentiate between normal erotic excitement and lust of the heart. He argued that God would certainly not have created beautiful people only to forbid anyone to notice them. Just because people may feel attracted to others in a physical or even sexual way does not imply that they have necessarily lusted or are guilty of sin.

It's critical to find an accurate and Biblical definition of sinful lust that separates basic human attraction from the deadly "adultery of the heart" that Jesus warned his disciples to avoid. Sinful lust simply cannot be the same as basic human attraction. There must be more to it than that. Smedes suggests:

> *"...there is a difference between the awareness of someone's sexual attractions and being dominated by a desire for that person's body... Attraction can become captivity; and when we have become captives of the thought, we have begun to lust. When the sense of excitement conceives a plan to use a person, when attraction turns into scheme, we have crossed beyond erotic excitement into spiritual adultery."* [13]

It is not sexual attraction, but *captivity* to sexual attraction that can become idolatry and take control of someone's life. Self-control, therefore, becomes a critical virtue for keeping desire from running amuck.

How, then, should "sinful lust" be defined? What's the bottom line in determining the difference between desire and "adultery of the heart?"

Answering these questions has been difficult for many who have simply equated lust with human sexual desire. Not only is that definition inaccurate, but it is damaging for believers who want to keep their hearts pure before God. For in trying to be pleasing to Him, sensitive, God-seekers often feel guilty because their physical desires, dreams, or fantasies do not go away. But praise be to God that all the desires that surface are not necessarily the true desires of my heart. Not every image, thought, or fantasy that passes through my mind finds its way into my heart. Sometimes the very act of imagining something (with all its consequences) is all it takes for me to completely reject a thought as inconsistent with my true heart's desire.

What is in my heart reflects my true priority. It is the thing that I want to do and will do if I have the opportunity. When a plan, a goal, a thought, or desire settles into the depths of my heart, I have already judged it and determined it to be of worth or of value to my life. My mind, however, is the place where that judgment takes place. Everything should go through the filter of the mind before it finds a home in the heart. So to say that everything going on in my mind has already been accepted and embraced by my heart is to completely misunderstand the difference between the two.

Desire and sinful lust is just not the same thing. As previously indicated, there is indeed a strategic "line" inside of me, within my soul. It separates mere mental activities from the priorities of my heart. The mind by itself is simply not the same thing as the heart. They are connected, but distinct. There is, absolutely, a line in the soul that separates the two. The important, foundational, "million dollar question" then is this: When does the vision of my eye or consideration of my mind settle into my heart and become part of who I am? Consider again Dr. Lewis Smedes' insightful definition of sinful lust:

> *"When the sense of excitement conceives a plan to use a person, when attraction turns into scheme, we have crossed beyond erotic excitement into spiritual adultery."* [14]

So to be classified as sinful, lust must lead to a "plan" or a "scheme," some kind of acting out of an unlawful desire or fantasy. At this point, the tempting image or thought has already taken root in the heart. Someone once said, "A bird can fly overhead, or even land on the branch without making a nest in the tree." Desire becomes sinful lust when arousal takes on a life of its own and "builds a nest" in the heart. Again, it's important to underscore the difference between sexual awareness, arousal, and sin. The Bible does not equate a healthy sexuality with sinful lust or adultery of the heart. Being sexual people, with sexual desires and thoughts does not necessarily produce the sinful lust of the heart that Scripture condemns. It is twisted action coming out of twisted priorities that gets people tangled up in sin. It is a heart that has been enticed and seduced that compromises holy standards and dances with the devil.

Many people believe it is impossible to "draw the line" between innocent attraction and sinful lust. I beg to differ. By the leading of the Holy Spirit, and through a proper understanding of Biblical teaching, even Christians with high sexual drives can keep themselves free from sinful lust. And because God's power is actively working within, sexual purity is not a "pie-in-the-sky dream" for followers of Jesus Christ, but the expected outcome of a Spirit-filled life!

Understanding the Scriptures

Sinful lust, at its core, is not an "eye" or "mind" issue, nor is it a hormonal battle; it is a condition of the heart. To clearly see the difference, it is critical to get an accurate picture of Jesus' teaching. We really don't need a Webster's Dictionary definition of lust based on common usage; we need a Biblical definition, guided by the Holy Spirit. What was Jesus' understanding of sinful lust? Consider this strong, often-quoted passage of Scripture:

> *"You have heard that it was said, 'Do not commit adultery.' But I tell you that anyone who looks at a woman lustfully has already committed adultery with her in his heart. If your right eye causes you to sin, gouge it out and throw it away. It is better for you to lose one part of your body than for your whole body to be thrown into hell. And if your right hand causes you to sin, cut it off and throw it away. It is better for you to lose one part of your body than for your whole body to go into hell."*
> *(Matthew 5:27-30)*

Three critical, illuminating points must be made to properly understand this teaching:

#1) *Jesus is revealing the reasons behind the commands*

Before we look at the specifics of what Jesus actually said, let's first get a bird's eye view of this famous sermon from which the comments come. We often refer to this message as Jesus' Sermon on the Mount. Jesus is revealing the heart and perspective of God by demonstrating that the Law of Moses is fulfilled through loving God and loving people. Some religious leaders were experts in the technical aspects of the law, but had no revelation of the loving purpose of the law. They were technically pure according to the Law – but unloving and uncaring individuals. Jesus condemned the way they kept people from truly seeing God. He said:

> *"Woe to you, teachers of the law and Pharisees,*

you hypocrites! You shut the kingdom of heaven in men's faces. You yourselves do not enter, nor will you let those enter who are trying to." (Matthew 23:13)

Because of the influence of their wicked teachers, many of the common people had misunderstood the whole point of the law. They had religion but no understanding of the heart of God. Jesus' teaching was both practical and simple – illuminating for the people the purpose behind the law, its reason for existence.

Jesus' teaching was not given to inaugurate some new system of Law or code of obedience, but to reveal the very heart of God behind the commands. He was not so much giving new moral directives as he was digging deeper into the real meat and original purpose of the Commandments. Even the statement, *"You have heard, but I say unto you..."* repeated frequently by Jesus in this sermon was the typical way Jewish teachers of the day would refer to the Law when they were describing its deeper meaning. Just like children as they mature need to know why certain regulations are in place, so Jesus was answering the "why" questions behind the Law. He was showing the reasons behind the rules by explaining that love for God and for others was actually the foundational principles upon which the entire Law was established.

Through his simple but radical message, Jesus was calling forth God-seekers (and still is!) who could perceive the eternal principles that inspired God to give his people the Law in the first place, and walk in the revelation of that truth. He was summoning people to go much deeper into the heart of God, challenging them to a greater degree of love, much more radical than simple observance of the Ten Commandments. As a matter of fact, in a couple instances, Jesus exhorts His followers in view of God's loving heart and original plan to go even beyond what the Law requires in serving people and keeping covenants (i.e. His comments on loving our enemies, restricting divorce and eliminating oaths with loopholes). Later on in the book of Matthew when an expert in the Law asked Jesus which was the Law's greatest command, he replied:

> *"Love the Lord your God with all your heart and with all your soul and with all your mind. This is the first and greatest commandment. And the second is like it: 'Love your neighbor as yourself.' All the Law and Prophets hang on these two commandments." (Matthew 22:37-40)*

These two greatest of commands were the foundation stones upon which the entire Law was built. Understanding and practicing this love of God would turn mere religion into life-giving relationships, legalism into love, and technical obedience of rules and regulations into tenderness, mercy and ministry towards others.

The Commandments were not disconnected, random rituals, but specific directives teaching people how to live in loving relationships with God and each other. Towards the end of the Sermon on the Mount, Jesus gave a remarkable conclusion often referred to as the "Golden Rule":

> *"In everything do to others what you would have them do to you, for this sums up the Law and the Prophets." (Matthew 7:12)*

The Sermon on the Mount was all about how to live in the love of God— How to glorify God by loving people with the supernatural resource of His love. It was about going the "extra mile" and loving others even when they did not deserve it. Jesus did not want his people simply being "technically righteous" and "law abiding," but lovers of people as well. He wanted his disciples to set the world on fire with the flame of God's love. Jesus' amplification of the Law, therefore, was an attempt to help people see the living principles behind every command and thereby act toward others in the spirit and not just in the letter of those principles.

#2- Jesus is specifically teaching against a form of adultery

For the people of Israel, the Law of Moses was clear - having sex with someone else's wife was wrong. Specifically, it was a sin against the woman's legitimate husband. That was the technical definition of adultery. Interestingly, having sex with an unmarried woman was not technically adultery. Penalties were in place for a man who had sex with an unmarried virgin who was still a part of her father's household (and therefore her father's property under Jewish Law), but this was not considered adultery. According to Jewish law, adultery actually occurred when an illicit sexual act was consummated between a man and a woman married to someone else. The Mathew passage is therefore specifically referring to a man who is pursuing another man's wife. Even the Greek word "*gune*," translated here "woman," could and in this case should be translated "wife."[15] This passage is specifically warning one man not to threaten the marriage of another by going after the other man's bride.

Jesus challenged some of the people's traditional way of thinking by claiming that it was not just intercourse with a married woman that was wrong, but even sexual advances towards her that made a man guilty of adultery. In other words, Jesus eliminated a major "loophole" some had used to justify their bad behavior. His words meant that a man who inappropriately made sexual advances towards another man's wife was already guilty of sin. His sinful behavior exposed a heart already corrupted by a spirit of adultery even before any actual sex occurred. Although the man was not technically (according to the Law of Moses) an adulterer if he had never actually taken the woman to bed; he was still, in God's eyes, guilty of sin.

This teaching from the Master revealed the heart of God's original command beyond its surface requirement. Jesus wanted the Jewish people to honor their word, their covenants, and their brother's property. In the ancient world women were definitely regarded as people, but also as property. Adultery was seen as a theft against the legitimate husband and his entire family. The one who "stole" a husband's "sexual property" (his wife) was not only coming between the husband and his wife, but also potentially robbing the entire family of legitimate heirs. For if a woman was caught in adultery, any child born later would be suspected of being illegitimate.

The reason Jesus makes dramatic statements about "cutting out the eye," or "cutting off the hand" was that both the eye and the hand were used in the plot to steal the woman's heart. A seductive look and an inappropriate touch made the eye and the hand the physical tools to work the evil of the heart. This kind of teaching was not unique to Jesus. The Babylonian Talmud (Jewish book of moral teaching) gives other examples of famous Jewish teachers using these same arguments, referring to eyes, hands, and feet that were responsible for adultery.[16] By referencing the eye and the hand, it becomes clear that Jesus was talking to the crowds about real external behavior as opposed to mere thoughts. He was specifically rebuking men for staring inappropriately at married women or touching them in a sexual way. He was pointing out that a persistent, lustful gaze and flirtatious, sexual touching of another man's wife was, in reality, the beginning stages of adultery. Even though actual sex may never occur, it was still a sin against the woman's husband, and an attack on their marriage covenant.

In Jesus' teaching, the man who compromises the marriage of another has a heart tainted by sin. He has acted out of a heart filled with sinful lust and a spirit of adultery. The lust is not there in his heart because of a night dream, a mental picture, or even a sexual fantasy. He is not guilty because of sexual desire, but because he has made a heart decision to pursue a sinful course of action by making unlawful sexual advances on someone else's wife. Even if he never fully succeeds in "going all the way," in Jesus' book, he is still an adulterer – maybe not physical adultery, but certainly an "adultery of the heart."

Up to this point we have been discussing the unlawful pursuit of married women. What about chasing after a married man, someone might ask? In Biblical times it was lawful for a man to have multiple wives, so unmarried women could legally pursue marriage to men that were already married. This is why the Law only referenced adultery as a sin which occurred with a married woman. In today's society, with polygamy outlawed in most places, adultery would obviously include illicit pursuit of a married man as well as chasing after a wedded wife.

Interestingly, however, this scripture really has nothing directly to say about courting or dating behavior between unmarried people. Many young people with hormones raging have been confused and discouraged by this passage. How can they even pursue a spouse in a godly way without becoming sexually aroused to some degree? And how can single people who are "looking" for a spouse keep from looking longingly into the eyes of someone with whom they are developing a loving relationship? Thankfully, Jesus was not outlawing arousal, desire, or dating. He was simply making the point that going after someone else's spouse was adultery from the start. It violated God's law of love by undermining a marriage covenant and stealing from someone else. But pursuing a romantic relationship with someone that is unmarried should not be considered wrong as long as it is free from manipulation or control and is properly submitted to godly counsel and authority.

#3 - Jesus is prohibiting actions – not thoughts

Many have interpreted the statements Jesus made about sinful lust as referring to the inner thought life of the believer. But the believer's inner thought life is not Jesus' specific concern in the Sermon on the Mount. As we pointed out earlier, His primary focus is on external behavior, the way people treat one another. "But wait," someone is thinking, "Jesus did in fact talk about the importance of heart attitudes." Well, yes he did. But according to the Lord, heart attitudes were unveiled or revealed by the way people acted towards one another. So Jesus was not simply talking about the thought life, but about heart attitudes that made people act certain ways.

Take, for instance, the discussion in the previous verses (Matthew 5:21-26) where Jesus was dealing with the subject of rage and anger. Here Jesus was trying to get the people to understand the importance of speaking and acting respectfully towards one other. Good Jews knew that murder was wrong, but often felt justified in stoning people with their words. Through his teaching, Jesus was digging deeper than the surface command of the Law and getting down to the real heart of the issue – or, should we say, the issues of the heart. According to the Lord, it was not just the *act* of murder that was wrong, but even *hateful behavior* towards someone else. Although an angry person may not go "all the way" and take someone else's life, verbally or physically abusing another person violates God's law of love. Hateful actions that violate this law of love prove that a person's heart has already been compromised and corrupted even though a physical act of murder may never take place. It is not, then, just extreme rage demonstrated through killing someone, but any hateful action coming from a wicked heart that Jesus calls sin. Again, in this case the Lord is not condemning angry thoughts, but hateful behavior.

This is "brand new" ground the Lord is breaking for much of his first-century Jewish audience. He is helping them to see that all ungodly behavior is wrong, even if it does not technically break one of the Ten Commandments. He is showing the people that the intents and attitudes of their hearts are important to God *because* they will definitely affect the way they treat others. The heart can't hide. It will ultimately show its true colors. Later in this same book Jesus says:

> *"For out of the overflow of the heart, the mouth speaks. The good man brings good things out of the good stored up in him, and the evil many brings evil things out of the evil stored up in him."* (Matthew 12:24-25)

Jesus frequently exposed the emptiness of following religious laws without ever really having a true change of heart. Regardless of how "religious" someone seems, bad behavior towards others uncovers a wicked, selfish heart. In contrast, pure religion (radical relationship with God) makes people loving and lovable. Good fruit comes off good trees! (Matthew 7:17) When a heart is truly changed, a person's actions will become consistently loving and nurturing to others. A change of heart brings a change of behavior. But a wicked heart, no matter how "religious" it may seem will continue to treat people disrespectfully. In Jesus' mind, you couldn't separate the heart from the way a person lives life and interacts with others. Bad behavior, therefore, exposes a sinful heart.

Redefining Sinful Lust

With this in mind we can now turn to the subject of sinful lust and better understand Jesus' approach. When teaching against "adultery of the heart," Jesus is speaking about unloving behavior that comes out of a selfish heart. Though someone may chase another person's spouse in the name of love, it is really nothing but covetousness – a desire to possess someone who belongs to another. For Jesus, the pursuit itself was considered sin in the eyes of God. He insisted that any flirtatious sexual behavior towards the wife of another man is sexual theft even if the illicit activity never makes it all the way into the bedroom. Outlawing "adultery of the heart" was not to make every erotic thought the same as sinful lust, or even to equate all fantasies with adultery, but to outlaw the inappropriate pursuit of a real person who was out-of-bounds and therefore unavailable.

Many people when referring to this passage in Matthew talk about the sin of "lust in the heart." Technically, "lust in the heart" is not even mentioned in this passage. Jesus is defining "adultery in the heart." He does mention the *"lustful look,"* but only as a manifestation of a deeper problem. His main concern is a heart bent towards adultery. The Lord is not teaching against sexual attraction or even mental imagining, but against a heart that covets another's spouse and makes a decision to pursue or to "act out" in some way.

The word "lustfully" in this passage is actually used to describe the word "looks," as opposed to thoughts. Its lustful looks, therefore, not sexual thoughts that Jesus is attacking. What exactly are the "lustful looks" that Jesus calls sin? Look again at the passage:

> *"You have heart that it was said, 'Do not commit adultery.' But I tell you that **anyone who looks at a woman lustfully** has already committed adultery with her in his heart." (Matthew 5:27-28)*

The Greek word translated "lustfully" here modifies "looks" and is a form of the word "*epithumeo,*" meaning "strong desire."[17] The word (in its various forms) is used frequently in the New Testament in both positive and negative contexts. In today's culture, we tend to use the word almost exclusively to describe something sexual. In the New Testament era, however, the word was used non-sexually as well as sexually. For example, Scripture uses the word positively and non-sexually when Jesus was said to have "lusted" (*epithumia*-strongly desired) to eat the Passover with His disciples. (Luke 22:15) Did you know Scriptures claimed that Jesus lusted?

In another instance, the Apostle Paul says that if a man desires the office of an Overseer, he "desires (*epithumei*) a noble task." (1 Timothy 3:1) What if your Pastor got up on Sunday and included "lust" in his sermon on the qualifications for church eldership!? Can you imagine the scandal? The next day the town would be buzzing, with people whispering and gossiping around their coffeepots and copiers talking about that weird church that requires its leaders to lust!

Obviously, the original word for lust was used much more widely and comprehensively than it is today. Even when the word was used negatively and in a sexual context, its meaning then was different from the way it is commonly used today. When used negatively in Scripture, the word literally meant "to covet."

In referring to the Ten Commandments, the Apostle Paul quoted the tenth commandment which said: "Thou shall not covet." (Romans 7:7) And yes, the Greek word Paul used here for "covet" was "*epithumian,*" another form of the same word translated "lustfully" back in the Sermon on the Mount. The negative, sinful application of this word is "to covet," to earnestly desire to posses something or someone that is "off-limits."[18] It was NOT sinful under the Ten Commandments to want to have something that wasn't yours. It was, however, wrong to so desire what someone else had, that you began to resent them, treat them rudely, or try in some way to take what rightfully belonged to them. Coveting became sinful when it negatively affected ones' attitude towards God or others. The same Greek word we have been researching (*epithumia*) is also used in the Greek translation of the Old Testament, the Septuagint, for the Tenth Commandment: "Thou shall not covet." The Septuagint was a Greek version of the Old Testament Scriptures often used by Jews during the time of Christ. In this Tenth Commandment, the Jews were specifically told that they were not to covet another man's spouse:

> *"You shall not to covet your neighbor's wife...or anything that belongs to your neighbor." (Deuteronomy 5:21)*

Jesus' comment, then, on "lustful looks" was not an entirely new concept, but really just a deeper look at the eternal principles behind the Law. Lust, when used in a negative way, is simply a heart that covets. In other words, a strong desire or commitment to possess and take something I should not have; specifically, that which belongs to someone else.

The word used in Matthew 5:28 is actually an adverb, "lustfully," describing *the way* someone looks at another. Many people miss this point when studying this text. Jesus is not talking about a thought in the mind, but a lustful look of the eye. This passage is not about thoughts, but about seductive activity. The Lord is not addressing a mental problem, but a behavioral one. What Jesus is prohibiting is a possessive or covetous glare that seeks to possess someone who is already taken. For an erotic, suggestive stare at someone who is off-limits uncovers a sinful, covetous heart that has already made a decision to pursue an illicit affair. I use the word "stare" deliberately because the Greek word for "looks" in this passage is the word *"Blepo"* which is not a quick look, but a protracted gaze.[19]

To sum it up then, the lustful look that the Lord denounces is a protracted, covetous, "I want you and I've got to have you," stare at someone who is married. It is a longing look which "undresses" the woman or man and sends all the wrong signals. It's not a look of admiration or appreciation of beauty that concerns the Lord, but a sexy, possessive stare at the wrong person with the purpose of erotic enticement. That is what Jesus is teaching against.

It is obvious that Jesus had in mind more than just a look, but an entire chase; a sinful, sexual pursuit of forbidden fruit. This becomes even clearer when you consider his remedy for the problem:

> *"If your right eye causes you to sin, gouge it out and throw it away. It is better for you to lose one part of your body than for your whole body to be thrown into hell. And if your right hand causes you to sin, cut if off and throw it away. It is better for you to lose one part of your body than for your whole body to go into hell." (Matthew 5:29-30)*

The Lord suggests that the guilty party should pluck out an eye and cut off the hand that causes sin. Though he was obviously using exaggeration and hyperbole to make a strong point, he was serious though about the sin of threatening marriage covenants by chasing married women. The pursuit beyond the look is strongly implied by his additional reference to the guilty hand. Improper sexual touching was obviously part of this unlicensed romance. As mentioned before, other Jewish Rabbis at the time of Jesus taught against "adultery of the hand."[20] The hand and sensual touching has always played a major role in human sexuality. Jesus was forbidding the improper, seductive use of touch to illegally entice someone married to another.

Sexual sin has always been a problem for mankind. Regardless of culture or ethnicity, mankind has always struggled with adultery. Some people mistakenly think that in back in "the good ole days" people did not have to deal with temptation like we do today. In ancient times, however, adultery was as strong an allurement as it is today. Often married women would be left alone as their husbands went off to battle or for business purposes. Their trips away from home would not consist of a few hours of outside work coupled with a short plane trip, but would entail a lengthy journey, sometimes lasting for several months. It was not uncommon for husbands and wives to find themselves separated for long periods of time. In light of this, Jesus was calling on the people of God to respect one another not only face to face, but "behind each other's backs" as well. When the husband was gone, his wife was off limits to other men. Not only off limits for sexual intercourse, but also for all sexual flirtation, pandering and pleasure.

As we conclude our survey of this scripture from the Sermon on the Mount, let's look again at the core of Jesus' teaching about sinful lust and adultery of the heart. His point is that for a person to be technically innocent of adultery, but yet to have a problem flirting with and pursuing someone else's spouse is to actually be guilty anyway. This is "adultery of the heart," an unloving, self-serving behavior absolutely unacceptable for God's people. The person who pursues illicit affairs in this way has already violated what love requires by threatening to steal from another. Potentially breaking up someone else's marriage is wrong from the moment the "scheme" begins.

Again, Jesus is concerned about actions, not simply attractions or thoughts. It's not a mind issue, but a heart problem exposed by covetous behavior. Sexual awareness, or even an erotic fantasy which is never acted upon in any way, is not being condemned by Jesus. Obviously, the thought life of the Christian must be judged and discerned, and ultimately submitted to the Spirit of God. (2 Corinthians 10) But in reality, it's the conviction and decision of the heart, not the image of the mind that determines behavior. As we have said before, the heart can't hide! It will ultimately show its' colors. How the agenda or plan of the heart reveals itself through actions toward others will unveil a person's true spiritual and moral condition. Every action counts, because every action towards another human being either supports or violates Jesus' Golden Rule of love. (Matthew 7:12)

The interpretation that I have suggested for Jesus' comments on the lustful look and adultery of the heart (Matthew 5:27-30) is the most consistent with the overall context and message of the Sermon on the Mount. Catholic Theologian, Gareth Moore, sees it the same way. In discussing this important passage Dr. Moore said:

> *"Jesus is not talking about inner thoughts divorced from action...thinking you want somebody when actually you don't...(but) about doing... taking or trying to take them."* [21]

Some might argue this to be a "liberal interpretation" because it is not the way many conservative Christians have understood the passage. Note, however, the comments on Matthew 5:28 from a conservative theologian, Dr. Craig L. Blomberg, in The New American Commentary, Volume 22:

> *"the present participle "blepon" refers to one who continues to look rather than just casting a passing glance, and in either case the mere viewing or mental imagining of a naked body is not under consideration. Instead, Jesus is condemn-*

ing lustful thoughts AND ACTIONS (emphasis mine) - those involving an actual desire (the most literal translation of the verb "epitymeo") to have sexual relations with someone other than one's spouse...." [22]

Although you may not recognize Dr. Blomberg's name, many will recognize the name of his publisher – *Broadman & Holman Publishers.* This company is the publishing arm of the Southern Baptist Church which has a reputation for being both theologically and socially conservative. This understanding, therefore, of what constitutes "adultery of the heart" is not only the best way to fit the discussion into the larger context of Jesus' sermon, but also is consistent with current scholarship both in Catholic and Protestant circles.

Some might argue that while the interpretation of the Matthew passage that I have suggested is feasible, there are still other passages of Scripture which clearly teach that it is wrong to focus on someone else's beauty or sex appeal. What about Job's statement often quoted?

"I have made a covenant with my eyes not to look lustfully at a girl." (Job 31:1)

Or how about in the wisdom of Proverbs where Scriptures warn young men to stay away from the ungodly woman saying:

"Do not lust in your heart after her beauty or let her captivate you with her eyes." (Proverbs. 6:25)

Both these Scriptures must be seen in their original context to be properly understood and applied. In Job's case, he was married (Job 31:10), and was talking about the sin of "lurking" at his neighbor's door" (31:9), that *is pursuing someone else's wife*! This becomes even clearer in his next statement as Job insists that if he were in fact guilty of this sin,

> *"... then may my wife grind another man's grain, and may other men sleep with her." (Job 31:10)*

In other words, Job was saying, "If I'm pursuing someone else's wife with the goal of having illicit sex with her, then may my own wife also sleep with another man."

Just as in Jesus' teaching, sinful lust (or covetousness) in Job's day was defined as an ungodly pursuit of another man's wife. Similarly, the Proverb mentioned earlier is also warning men about the danger of being seduced by a woman who is married to someone else. Immediately before commanding the young man, *"Do not lust after her beauty,"* the writer defines whom he is talking about by calling her *"an immoral woman...a wayward wife."* (Proverbs 6:24) The context of Proverbs six is a story of forbidden love where an unhappy homemaker is trying to sexually entice a young man to make love to her while her husband is away. The writer of Proverbs is communicating wisdom and common sense to the young man by reminding him that the husband will come back and most likely find out about the illicit affair. He says:

> *"For jealously arouses a husband's fury, and he will show no mercy when he takes revenge." (Proverbs. 6:34)*

In each of these passages of Scripture I have discussed, the issue being addressed is the importance of respecting and honoring one another's marriages. With a single voice, the Bible condemns the man who violates the marriage covenant of another by attempting or accomplishing "sexual theft."

A Fresh Perspective

What does all this mean for Christians today? All of us can certainly say a hearty "Amen" to Jesus' exhortation to respect and honor our marriage covenants. We are also inspired by the Master's words to continually examine our hearts and the underlying motives for our behavior. But there is also another side to this. Like it or not, new clarity on the true meaning of these Scriptures actually makes some issues a bit "grayer." Sometimes greater clarity about truth clouds up our nice, tidy, religious approaches to things. New Testament truth often pulls the rug out from under religiosity and forces us to delve into the heart of the matter and hear God for ourselves.

If sinful lust and adultery of the heart are to be defined as we have suggested, then there needs to be some paradigm shifts, changes in our thinking regarding our basic understanding of what constitutes sinful lust. These changes in thinking may alter to some degree our perception of right and wrong.

In the 1970's President Jimmy Carter created quite a stir when he confessed to a reporter of *Playboy* magazine that he committed adultery "often"! What he meant was that according to his understanding of sinful lust, he was guilty many times over of "adultery of the heart." Most likely, our sensitive President was not in fact guilty on a daily basis of coveting the wives of other men. He simply experienced normal erotic reactions (and possibly thoughts) which are common for normal heterosexual men when they get in the presence of beautiful women.

Authors Robert and Mollie Brow make some insightful comments about this subject:

> *Since it was the Son of God himself who designed feminine beauty, we can't imagine that Jesus would fault men for finding women attractive.*

John 1:1-3 and Colossians 1:13-16 both tell us that the Jesus who appeared on earth was the eternal Son of God who designed our world, and that must have included inventing and implanting our sexual instincts. So we cannot believe that Jesus is condemning the appreciation of another's beauty when there is no intention to engage in the physical act of adultery. In Galilee Jesus enjoyed the company of women and men, and loved them intensely without anyone ever suggesting that he sinned in doing so. But if he was fully man, and tempted in all points as we are (Hebrew 4:11), he cannot have escaped sexual temptation. The text "But I say to you that everyone who looks at a woman with lust has already committed adultery with her in his heart" (Matthew 5:28) is about adulterating a marriage. And the point is that from God's point of view adultery has already occurred when THE DECISION (emphasis mine) to be unfaithful has been made...Zealous preachers have often confused enjoying the beauty of a person of the opposite sex with lust. But enjoyment is not a fault. As we pass a neighbor's garden we can stop to enjoy the beauty and even smell the fragrance of a carnation without being tempted to cut it and take it home."[23]

The Brow's have beautifully summed up a major point we have been making so far: Inappropriate sexual lust is not an attraction, thought, fantasy or desire, but is instead "adultery of the heart" – a scheme played out in real life which undermines the integrity of someone else's marriage covenant. The difference between these two understandings is significant. It is not the mind, then, but the heart that becomes the real culprit in sinful lust. As we pointed out before: It is when innocent attraction births a scheme or a plan to use, abuse or defile another that sinful lust actually comes to life. At that point, we are no longer talking about normal sexual attraction, but a heart problem. It becomes a sin of the heart, literally, "adultery of the heart," and is an abomination to God.

The Bible condemns covetousness of all kinds. Sinful lust is really nothing more than an ugly covetousness in one's heart that affects the way he or she treats others. It covets what it does not have that belongs to someone else. Whether it's another person's spouse or possessions, covetousness becomes a problem when an appreciation and admiration of what belongs to my neighbor becomes an obsession for me to attain.

If the Bible has, in fact, been often misunderstood, and there needs to be some paradigm shifts in our thinking, what then changes? I submit that the most dramatic shift is one that turns human sexual behavior from a list of rules and regulations to an examination of the heart and an ear to hear what the Spirit is saying. For instance, if these passages we have examined so far speak primarily about honoring marriage covenants, then what about singles' sexuality? Also, if "lust" is only wrong when acted upon in some way, how does this potentially change our understanding of sexual purity?

We will examine these issues and more as we continue looking into this hot subject in the pages of this book. For now, suffice it to say that many Christians are misapplying the scriptures we have examined and using them to enforce rigid dating regulations for singles or to police the inner thought life of believers. Doing this often results from taking the Scriptures out of context and misunderstanding them. Many rules, regulations, and guilty consciences have been created through misinterpretation. Clarifying what "adultery in the heart" really is and what it is not should be an important key to unlocking bared doors and setting many captive Christians free from jails of condemnation. This newfound clarity should also help us get our focus on what is really important to God – integrity, covenant-keeping, and respect for one another, rather than spend our time swimming aimlessly, lost in a confusing sea of conflicting religious ideas.

CHAPTER 4

Sexy on Sundays?

She had just moved to the south from New York City. Excited to be living now in a place where most of her new neighbors also attended church, this beautiful twenty-something recent convert sang in her car as she approached the well-known evangelical church. After bustling through the lobby, the young woman took a seat close to the front; she didn't want to miss a thing! Then it happened: An older woman with a badge on approached her from behind, tapped on her shoulder and requested that she meet her in the restroom. Wondering what was going on, the new Christian left her seat quickly and rushed to the back. Was someone hurt? Was someone looking for her? "Excuse me, honey," the older woman said, "maybe we can find a little sweater or something to put over your shoulders. That strapless is showing just a little too much skin." Dumbfounded and embarrassed the new Christian found her way to the door and never came back.

Believe it or not, that scenario happens over and over again in conservative churches of all stripes. Sometimes it is "official church policy," other times it's just legalistic busy-bodies doing their own thing. Either way, situations like this beg the question: Is it ok to be sexy on Sunday?

Since inappropriate sexual lust is not sexual awareness or attraction, defining it in terms of what people think, what they wear, or how they react to what others wear is simply inaccurate. Many male preachers in their "fight against lust" have blamed women as the source of the problem because of what they wear (or don't wear!) Throughout the years of my pastoral ministry I have found that both men and women complain about how their brothers and/or sisters dress, particularly in church. It is interesting to me that many times what is criticized is attire that is common and considered appropriate outside church walls.

It seems that for some people, it's as if there are massive demons of lust that we all succumb to every day. And if we can just get an hour or two on Sundays to be free from their pervasive power, then we can have some sort of victory and sense of peace. I submit to you that we don't have to live on the run. If our conclusions in this study are correct, then many people are not committing sinful lust nearly as much as they might think! The enemy is using our misconceptions to attack and accuse us. "Religion" often produces traditions that become resources for Satan to use to undermine God's purpose and His people. I believe many of our "lust concerns" and "modesty issues" are these kinds of traditions that our enemy uses to confuse and distract us. Women do not cause men to lust by what they wear. Nor do men cause women to lust. As Jesus said,

> *"Nothing outside a man can make him unclean by going into him. Rather, it is what comes out of a man that makes him unclean...For from within, out of men's hearts, come evil thoughts, sexual immorality..." (Mark 7:15)*

Jesus, again, is pointing to the defective heart as the

source of evil. In Hebrew thought the heart was the organ of decision. As we observed earlier, it's a decision or a scheme to act in a covetous or lustful way that ushers in sin, not a reaction to a beautiful woman or a handsome man. According to Jesus, it is NOT what comes into us externally, but the decisions we make internally that potentially corrupt us. While sexy clothes may be an inappropriate distraction in a church service, they are not, however, creating lust in the hearts of worshippers.

But what about modesty, someone may ask? Doesn't scripture teach that women must dress modestly? Yes, it does. But just like the word "lust," the word "modesty" has come to mean something to many of us that it may not have meant to the authors of the Biblical texts. The subject is brought up by Apostle Paul in his first pastoral letter to Timothy, his "son in the faith" who was a young apostle overseeing the church in Ephesus. Paul told Timothy he wanted "women to dress modestly..."(1 Timothy 2:9) The word "modestly" used here by Paul to describe proper attire for women is a form of the Greek word *"kosmios"* which simply means "orderly."[24] It had a secondary meaning, "decorous,"[25] suggesting that the woman should "make herself beautiful in an orderly or appropriate way."

Paul was not encouraging the women to look ugly and unattractive, but beautiful and self-confident. The word does not reference sexuality. Paul simply requested that women dress appropriately. He was not concerned that they looked too sexy, but that some of the women were going overboard with extravagance or "gaudiness" in their worship attire. This is plainly obvious in the next verse where Paul encourages Christian women not to focus on *"expensive* clothes" but on "good deeds." (1 Timothy 2:10) Paul did not want the churches under his care to become overly concerned about *externals*, but on *internal* beauty and *eternal* truth.

Paul was determined, as was also the Apostle Peter, that

Christian women understand that their worth, significance, and lasting beauty come from within and not from external dress. Consider Peter's similar exhortation to women:

> *"Your beauty should not come from outward adornment...Instead, it should be that of your inner self, the unfading beauty of a gentle and quiet spirit, which is of great worth in God's sight. For this is the way the holy women of the past who put their hope in God used to make themselves beautiful..." (1Peter 3:3a, 4, 5a)*

As caring and concerned spiritual fathers, Apostles Paul and Peter wanted their sisters in Christ to perceive that real beauty was more than skin deep. These leaders were encouraging women to focus on inner beauty. Such is a beauty any woman can possess regardless of her body shape, age, or looks. It is not based upon outward appearance, or fancy clothes that money can buy, but upon a heart submitted to God; that is the source of true beauty. These early church leaders were concerned that worship services not become "fashion shows" where the rich and beautiful showed off their wares, but a time for pure fellowship with God and with one another.

Paul emphasized this same principle in dealing with a similar situation in his letter to the church at Corinth. He warned the Corinthians that their celebrations of the Eucharist (Lord's Supper) were not pleasing to the Lord because:

> *"Each of you goes ahead without waiting for anybody else. One remains hungry, another gets drunk!" (1 Corinthians 11:21)*

He reminded them that they had their own homes to eat

and drink in; but when they came together for Christian communion and fellowship, they needed to be more sensitive to the presence of the Lord and to one another. Some scholars believe that part of Corinth's problem was that rich believers were bringing plenty of food for themselves while the poor had little to eat and were going hungry.

If this was the case, the situation was similar in principle to what was going on in Ephesus regarding women's clothes. As we discussed earlier, Paul admonished Timothy to direct the women to dress modestly and not with "expensive clothes." (1 Timothy 2:10) Perhaps he was concerned that while some women were rich and could dress "to the hilt" in Timothy's church, others were poor and would possibly feel ashamed. As in Corinth, a damaging rift or division could emerge between the rich and the poor. Class distinction was a real problem in the first-century. Paul was working hard to eliminate such distinctions within the body of Christ.

In both the Ephesian church and the church at Corinth, the Apostle Paul was concerned that believers be sensitive to one another, relate lovingly, and eliminate anything that could be potentially divisive. His concern about modesty, therefore, had little or nothing to do with sexual lust. He simply was against inappropriate or gaudy dress that could potentially cause hard feelings or distraction interfering in the believers worship and ministry one to another.

Some of the other Greek words Paul uses in his instructions to Timothy about women's attire suggest that he may have also been concerned that some of the Christian women were dressing like the so-called "sacred prostitutes" of the pagan religions. It was the common custom for the prostitutes to weave gold ornaments into their braided hair.[26] These prostitute priestesses would have sexual intercourse in and around pagan temples with strangers to channel spiritual power and perform religious rituals in behalf of the deities that they worshipped. Some of these new Christians had probably been involved in some way with temple prostitution; many of the men had likely engaged in sexual relations inside the pagan temples, and some of the women may have served as temple prostitutes. Paul was concerned that the new converts make a clean break from this kind of idolatry.

The so-called "sacred sex" phenomena was definitely practiced in ancient Ephesus[27] and was likely happening when Paul wrote his letter to Timothy regarding the church in that region.

Paul was also concerned about this same bizarre behavior with the church at Corinth. Historically, that ancient city had a reputation far and wide as a center of sexual promiscuity. So-called "sacred sex" seems to have been one of its favorite pastimes. History records that during its heyday over 1000 "prostitute priestesses" were serving as "ministers" in one temple alone![28]

For the church living in Corinth where this ancient demonic stronghold existed, Christian women were allowed to prophesy and minister publicly, but only with proper reverence and symbolic head covering (1 Corinthians 11:5). This was to separate these women from the way the priestesses of the pagan religions dressed (or undressed!) and functioned. As opposed to the sexual manipulation and exploitation that the pagan women used in worship, Christian women were to draw attention off themselves and onto the Lord. They were allowed, even encouraged to minister, but in a way that separated their style and approach from the women who led worship in the temples.

Understanding the situation in these Greco-Roman cities helps us to better understand and appreciate Paul's admonition to women about what they wear. It also helps us to translate the term, *"decency,"* the next word used in 1 Timothy 2:9 to describe the proper dress for Christian women:

"I also want women to dress modestly, with decency and propriety..." (1 Timothy 2:9)

The Greek word for decency is *"aidos,"* used only one other time in the New Testament. Its other occurrence is in Hebrews 12:28, where the word is translated "reverence." Again, the Apostle Paul was not putting down the women (as is implied in the old King James translation of the word as "shamefacedness"); instead he simply desired that Christian women be dressed in ways that would glorify God and not some pagan deity. He did not want other worshippers distracted or confused by women dressing like the infamous temple prostitutes. None of the detrimental pagan worship practices or beliefs was going to find their way into the young Christian community on Paul's watch!

The other key word used in this verse to describe how women should dress was *"sophrosune"* in the Greek, translated "propriety" in the NIV. The word simply means "with soundness of mind" or "good judgment."[29] The word implies that the woman gives care, and even prayer to what she wears. She is to use maturity and good judgment to put on what is appropriate for the particular context in which she finds herself.

This point serves as an excellent conclusion to understanding the Apostle Paul's thinking regarding the subject of women's attire. *His concern was that every woman use spiritual discernment to make sure that her outfit did not honor some false god or false concept of spirituality, compete with her sister in Christ, or become a counterfeit source of beauty and identity for her as a person.* Worship assemblies were not supposed to be about clothes anyway, but were times to reverence the Lord and minister to one another.

It's also important to keep in mind that these people whom Paul was addressing were his spiritual children, under his spiritual care. Speaking as their father in the faith, he felt he needed to give practical instruction to his "kids" and emphasize the true spiritual reasons why believers gather together in the first place. In doing so he deemphasized fashions, fads, and just plain foolishness that could possibly distract and take people's focus off the Lord.

Seeing the "big picture" helps to make sense out of these scriptures which are so often misunderstood and misapplied. In the first-century churches that Apostle Paul governed, the guidelines given for women's dress were primarily to distinguish them from idolatry and diminish any ungodly competition over fashion, not to protect men from lust.

These passages have very little, if anything, to do with ungodly, sexual lust. Yet in today's common terminology, words like "modesty" always seem to be used to refer to our sexuality. In contemporary Christian lingo, a modest person is one who covers up skin. But when we read our modern definitions of certain words back into these ancient texts, we can completely miss the point.

Perhaps it could be said that these scriptures *indirectly* speak to what we typically call modesty today. For instance, women (and men) certainly need to be aware that they are not distracting worshippers by what they wear. Most sincere Christians would understand the importance and necessity of that. But to say that a woman is sinning, or causing men to sin, because she looks sexy is to read something into the passage that is just not there. It also uncovers a misunderstanding about the true nature of sinful lust. People should be able to notice other beautiful people and admire their beauty without feeling guilty. The Bible does not call that sin.

If you feel some sense of attraction when encountering a beautiful person, perhaps you should be encouraged instead of feeling filthy. Be encouraged that you are hormonally balanced and sexually healthy; not everyone is. Sexuality, including sexual attraction, is a gift given by God. By His grace we can learn both to enjoy it and to control it. Thanks be to God that sexuality does not have to be "cast out" for us to be holy.

Looking at the "big picture" it is also important to note that it is not Spirit-filled, grace-oriented Christianity that emphasizes the hiding and covering up of the human body, but a radical, fundamentalist form of Islam instead. In the name of modesty, some of these repressive zealots demand that nothing feminine or sexually defining in a woman's physique ever be seen in public. One Muslim moderator recently explained in an important conference that one of the main reasons radical Muslims despise American Christianity as they do is because of the way women's bodies are allowed to be displayed.

Christians should be on the other side of that fence. We should stand with women, believing that their beauty and femininity should be celebrated, not hidden. It is demeaning to women to suggest that they are dangerous, poisonous, and somehow threatening to men. It is simply inaccurate to say that a woman's dress causes men to behave badly. If a man takes advantage of a woman because of how she is dressed, the real problem is not in her attire, but in his heart.

Honestly, the underlying issue, especially in repressive religious systems, is that many men are uncomfortable with the way women make *them* feel. Quite frankly, it's a scary thing to some men. Because they feel somewhat sexually vulnerable or even threatened by women, these guys believe they must "keep women down." Because of male ego on the one hand and insecurity on the other, some men look at emerging, self-confident, successful, sexy women as the enemy.

For many reasons living Christianity should not borrow from fundamentalist Muslim dress codes. I'm not just speaking of the wearing of veils and body coverings, but the principles that are behind that kind of thinking.

God made the human body and called it "very good." He

also created us as sexual beings. We are not to fear the body or be afraid of sexual awareness and attraction. Sexual attraction and sinful lust is not the same thing. If I were to live my life fearing the human body and sexual attraction, I could never go to a public beach again. As a matter of fact, I couldn't even walk through public malls! There has got to be a better way.

Through our international ministry we oversee churches in the wonderful South American nation of Brazil. Brazil boasts some of the most beautiful beaches and people in the world. Because of its heat and culture, many of the Brazilian people wear less clothing than their North American counterparts. Beachwear tends to be more revealing as well. In one city there is a group of very traditional, legalistic churches that don't come to the beach with the general public, but will venture out into the water during their yearly convention. At the appointed time, the people converge on the beach as a group. The men are in suits and ties, the women in long dresses. The locals of the area come out in droves to watch the "crazy Christians" have their annual beach experience. What saddens me is that instead of being known for their love, compassion, acts of kindness, intimacy with God, or incredible miracles, many of these Christians are simply known for their legalism and fear of seeing the human body.

Thank God that lust is not defined by what the body wears, or the eye sees, but by what comes out of the heart, or will of man. Remember, again, this incredible insight from the Master:

> *"Listen to me, everyone, and understand this.*
> *Nothing outside a man can make him 'unclean' by*
> *going into him. Rather, it is what comes out of a*
> *man that makes him 'unclean'...What comes out*
> *of a man is what makes him 'unclean.' For from*

*within, **out of men's hearts**,(emphasis mine) come evil thoughts, sexual immorality, theft, murder, adultery, greed, malice, deceit, lewdness, envy, slander, arrogance and folly. All these evils come from inside and make a man 'unclean.' (Mark 7:14, 20-23)*

It is not simply what the eye sees or the mind thinks that makes a person "unclean." Instead it is evil intentions coming from the heart that lead to bad behavior and bring spiritual pollution into someone's life. This bad fruit comes from a heart that is self-centered and unloving towards others. The mind is not the culprit; that's simply where we examine and consider our options. The heart is where attitudes are formed and decisions are made.

Jesus did say "evil thoughts" come from a defective heart. He was not, however, talking about random thoughts in our minds, but decisions of the heart. This is more apparent in the original Greek than it is in our English translations. The Greek word used here for "evil thoughts" is *"dialogismos,"* which can also mean "arguments."[30] (see also 1 Timothy 2:8; Philippians 2:14 Romans 14:1; and 1 Corinthians 3:20) Jesus was not simply talking about our thought life, but about devious plans or even destructive conversations that could damage others. For the Jewish people, the heart was seen as the "organ of decision."

The overall point Jesus was making in this text was that people can not blame their sin on external forces. Covetousness or lust does not come upon me because of what someone else wears or has; it comes instead from a heart decision to possess what I should not have, regardless of the consequences.

CHAPTER 5

Mind Games

If the definition of sinful lust that I have proposed in this book is accurate (and I think that it is), then what really displeases God is covetous desire coming from a selfish heart. A desire to acquire gone bad, resulting in egocentric behavior that abuses real people in real situations and treats them in a negative, "un-Christ-like" way. If this is forbidden sexual lust, rather than feeling sexual attraction or even experiencing sexual thoughts, is it ok then for us as Christians to dream up whatever sexual fantasies we might imagine? Obviously not. Paul says,

> *"You, my brothers, were called to be free. But do not use your freedom to indulge the sinful nature; rather serve one another in love" (Galatians 5:13)*

Any fantasy, for instance, that uses or abuses another human being is not consistent with the "royal law of love" (James 2:8) we are called to obey and must be rejected. The Apostle Paul commented in his second letter to the Corinthians:

*"...we take every thought captive and make it obe-
dient to Christ." (2 Corinthians 10:5)*

Paul was not saying that only "spiritual thoughts" will
continually fill our minds. The point he was making is that as
Spirit-filled believers we should allow the Holy Spirit to discern our thought life and reveal any place where we could be
believing a lie or slipping into unbelief. We are called to
demolish "strongholds" and "arguments" (2 Cor.10:4-5). In
other words, we are not to let the enemy control our minds
with his perspective and agenda. Instead, we should "have
our minds set on what the Spirit desires." (Romans 8:5) The
Holy Spirit of God will work with our minds to evaluate what
part of our inner thought life is worthwhile and what is not.
As He judges and discerns, we then listen to His inner voice
and begin to make heart decisions; pursuing the dreams and
visions that are truly from Him and throwing out anything
that would ultimately be hurtful to God, others, or ourselves.

Someone may ask: "What then about this silly, even
slightly-erotic fantasy that is not negatively impacting my
heart, my understanding of God's will for my life, or my
relationship with others? Is it wrong?"

Consider these words from Richard J. Foster in his book,
The Challenge of the Disciplined Life:

*"...the first thing that believers should do is to
refuse to bear the heavy burden of self-condemna-
tion for every erotic image that floats through
their minds. Sometimes sexual fantasies signify a
longing for intimacy; at other times, they express
attraction toward a beautiful and winsome person. Sexual fantasies can mean many things, and
we must not automatically identify them with lust.
It is also helpful to recognize the positive function
of fantasy. Through fantasy we are able to hold*

reality at bay while we allow the imagination to roam freely. Mature people are able to utilize the imagination without ever losing touch with the real world..."[31]

Lewis Smedes agrees in principle with Foster but adds this word of warning:

"Fantasy life can be treacherous. If we retreat too often into that world without risks, without demands, and without disappointments, it can become an escape from genuine encounter with real people. There is something tempting about fantasy life when real life is either dull or difficult. For people who habitually run away from reality that is less than perfect into the world where they can make everything turn out just as they want, there is real danger. But the danger is not that of lusting so much as of unfairness to the real people who populate our real world of sexual relationships."[32]

The main point, for mature believers, is to allow the Holy Spirit to lead and direct our lives. Our thought life, like everything else in our world, should be judged by and guided by the Spirit of God within us.

As a pastor, I become concerned for Christian people when I see them living in extremes. On the one hand, some do not handle fantasy well and become trapped in it. On the other hand, some have taken on so much guilt for sexually-oriented day dreaming or night dreaming that they feel completely defeated. Consider this perspective from authors Robert and Mollie Brow:

"Sexual fantasy was until very recently condemned

in all churches. The theory was that thinking impure thoughts would inevitably lead to sinful acts. Any kind of sexual fantasizing was therefore sinful. The result is that children picked up the idea that sexual thoughts are dirty, harmful, or downright wicked. A huge amount of guilt has resulted in the lives of young and not so young people. The inability to cope with sexual fantasies without feeling defiled makes it very hard for both men and women to handle the fantasies that intrude in the best of relationships...there is no need to condemn married and unmarried persons who have fantasies about exotic situations and persons without any intention to translate the fantasy into adultery. If we correctly interpreted Jesus' words about the point when a decision becomes adultery, it seems the same principle could be applied to sexual fantasy. And it makes no difference whether we enjoy a fantasy in a book or we create it ourselves. A fantasy, which if expressed in practice would be morally wrong, is not adulterous unless the will is harnessed to doing that particular act. What is important is that every kind of fantasy, including the sexual ones, should be brought to the Holy Spirit for evaluation." [33]

While some may believe the Brows have gone too far in what they allow, it is important to emphasize a very important point they are making. Many sincere Christians struggle under a tremendous weight of guilt that has hindered their spiritual development because they have not been able to stop thinking sexual thoughts.

Many if not most men who have confessed sin to me in confidence over the years confess a perceived struggle with lust. I recall one Sunday morning a precious, godly, eighty-year old man, happily married for over fifty years, confessing to me that he was "lusting" after women. Another more serious and even sadder confession was a single man in his late thirties who shared with me that he had to wear a "catcher's cup" (a sports protection devise) under his clothes to keep himself from becoming aroused. Was it really sinful lust these men were struggling with, or just an inability to spiritually understand, accept, or relate to their own sexuality? Do sexual thoughts or even fantasies that are never acted upon constitute sinful lust? According to our research in this book, many of them do not.

Now obviously, some people are genuinely *addicted* to pornography and sexual fantasy. It is important that in proclaiming freedom to some, we don't rationalize bondage in others. Addictions (of any kind) are idolatry for the Christian. Some Christians have "pet" addictions that have become the thief, robbing from their spiritual inheritance. Such addictions are serious and sometimes demand radical steps to be taken to break their controlling power. Much good literature has been written in the last ten years to help people get free from sexual bondage and addiction. It is important, however, to realize that not everyone is clinically addicted to sexual stimuli. For every Christian to treat his or her sexuality as if they were an addict can potentially create undue guilt and shut down healthy sexual self-perception, awareness and response.

The same principle also applies with other addictions. If a man has a "computer addiction" (which is very real in our present high-tech environment), he may need to completely get off-line and pack up the computer for a period of time. Serious problems with addiction demand that serious steps be taken to get free. Someone else, however, may not actually be "addicted" but become convicted that he is spending too much time on the computer. His strategy is simply to cut back on the amount of time spent "surfing the net" and writing E-Mails. Different approaches are called for depending on how strong the addiction has become. In the same way, if a man or woman becomes *controlled* by sexually oriented pictures, thoughts, books, magazines, fantasies, or even feelings, then a line has been crossed. Normal sexual desire has become sexual addiction, and a door has been opened to Satan. From that place he then develops a "foothold," gaining access to their lives, tormenting them and holding them back from their God-given destiny.

Sexual addiction is definitely a problem today, but not every sexual appetite invariably leads to this kind of bondage. It is simply inaccurate to assume that every sexually oriented dream or desire implies that one struggles with sexual addiction. When a healthy man goes for any length of time without an ejaculation, he will often become more sexually sensitive. While some traditionalists will claim that every sexual day-dream or night-dream comes from the devil, there may be a much more natural explanation. The dream or fantasy may simply come from seminal buildup, the accumulation of sperm needing and wanting to be released. After a "wet dream," masturbation, or a sexual encounter occurs, biological and psychological pressure subside in a man and his thought life often becomes less sexually charged than it was before. The woman may not have the same biological need for sexual release, but recent research has indicated that women have much greater overall sexual desire and need for orgasm than previously thought.

How many great men and women of God have sat in the back pews, watching their spiritual world go by because they felt defiled by their own sexuality? While some may pollute their thought world by planning and acting upon unlawful passions and desires, many more are riddled with guilt that they should not be carrying. Through better understanding of Scripture and the anointing of the Holy Spirit, God wants us to know that we possess victory in Him.

Remember, the key to dealing successfully with the thought life is to be in continual connection and communication with the Holy Spirit. He will serve as the "policeman" of our minds, telling us what to receive or reject, and will become the ultimate builder and establisher of God's priority within our hearts.

Every Christian is unique and must receive individual direction from the Lord. Obviously, that direction will often come through others who have been given authority over our lives, (Hebrew 13:7, 17) or even "spiritual peers" that we trust to help us properly discern the Lord's voice. But even with godly "checks and balances" in place, it is still obvious, for those who discern accurately, that what God allows (or even directs) some to do, is just not acceptable for others. Many people dislike the relativity of such an approach, but it's definitely Biblical. In Romans 14, regarding food regulations Paul said:

> *"I am fully convinced that no food is unclean in itself. But if anyone regards something as unclean, then for him it is unclean...So whatever you believe about these things keep between yourself and God. Blessed is the man who does not condemn himself by what he approves. But the man who has doubts is condemned if he eats, because his eating is not from faith; and everything that does not come from faith is sin. (Rom 14:14, 22-23)*

The point, then, is that I should submit my life to God and let Him give me clarity in my own heart about what is appropriate or not appropriate for me. This includes understanding and relating to my sexual appetite. He knows me best and can help me to understand "how I tick" and how I can best function, serving Him and walking victoriously in the midst of the particular life circumstances I have inherited. If my thoughts, dreams, fantasies, and actions are "walked out" to the glory of God, and if I sense His pleasure or release, then there is not a problem. On the other hand, if I feel convicted, and see "bad fruit" coming out of my inner thought life, then I need to repent and ask Him for new direction and strategy. The key principle is that whatever I do in my life, I should do it all to the glory of God (Colossians 3:27), submitting my life to the direction and control of His faithful and ever-present Spirit.

CHAPTER 6

"Sexual Solitaire" and Self-control

It has got to be one of the most hotly debated subjects in Christianity today. Just a few years ago, no one would even say the word out loud. Now that it is "out of the closet" a furious debate is underway in Christian circles. Some claim it is sin, others believe it to be a gift from God and key to self-control. Many others are confused and somewhere in the middle. What is this formerly forbidden word – masturbation. And it is not a peripheral subject, but one of universal relevance - practically everybody does it or has done it at one time. Studies have demonstrated that masturbation is not just the practice of a few over-sexed teenage boys or immodest girls. It seems to be almost everyone's issue at some point in time. Unfortunately, few Christian leaders have given clear-cut Biblical teaching on this red hot topic. James McCary, author of *Human Sexuality*, has found that about 95% of men and between 50% and 90% of women masturbate.[34] In his recent book, *The Sexual Man*, Fuller seminary Professor and Psychologist Dr. Archibald Hart reported that among 600 men surveyed, mostly from conservative religious backgrounds including many who were preparing for the ministry, masturbation was practiced by

the majority. Even among those married, 61% of this very
select, godly group of men admitted that they still masturbate.[35]

Church tradition since the middle ages has not been kind
to masturbation. Some church fathers taught that it was actually worse than extra-marital heterosexual intercourse and
incest because it was "unnatural" – against God's procre-
ative purpose for sex.[36] Even in the middle Ages the church
viewed any non-procreative emission of male sperm as dirty
and sinful. An ancient church writing, ***The Penitential of
Theodore,*** prescribed certain acts of penance for men who
waked to discover they had experienced a "wet dream", a
discharge of sperm during their sleep. The doctrine stated
that such a man must get out of bed immediately and sing
seven psalms of repentance. As if that wasn't enough, the
next morning he was told to sing thirty more! In the case that
the "pollution" had occurred as a result of falling asleep in
church, then the poor guy had to recite the entire book of
Psalms![37]

In the late 1800's the medical community around the
world jumped on the anti-masturbation bandwagon.
Thinking the loss of semen adversely affected the brain and
nervous system, medical journals in both Europe and
America were attaching almost every conceivable medical
problem to masturbation which they called "self-pollution"
or the "secret vice." The superintendent of the Massa-
chusetts Lunatic Asylum in 1848 claimed that during that
year 32% of the patients were admitted to the asylum for
"self-pollution" (masturbation).[38] In the south, the New
Orleans Medical Journal quoted a French doctor who said:

> *"In my opinion, neither the plague, nor war, nor
> smallpox, nor a crowd of similar evils have
> resulted more disastrously for humanity than the
> habit of masturbation. It is the destroying element*

of civilized society."[39]

Why would legitimate medical officials made such ridiculous claims? Well, these old-fashioned doctors actually had very little medical knowledge compared to what we know today. Their diagnosis and treatment of illness often bordered on the bizarre. Records show that these doctors attempted to treat sicknesses by draining blood out of their patients (bloodletting), forcing them to vomit, or blistering their skin.[40]

The so-called "sickness" of masturbation was sometimes treated by applying acid solutions or even leeches to the genitals to suck out the blood. One crazy doctor, A.J. Block of New Orleans, called female masturbation a "moral leprosy," and "treated" it on at least one occasion by removing a young girl's clitoris.[41] As strange as all of this sounds to modern ears, even as late as the 20th century, books were being written by moralists who claimed that masturbation could make one go insane.

Needless to say, the medical community has long since abandoned its crusade against masturbation. Misunderstandings about masturbation went the way of bloodletting and leech attachment. Finally, in 1972 the American Medical Association issued a long overdue medical analysis and declared masturbation a normal sexual activity. Some recent medical studies have actually argued that masturbation is physically and psychologically beneficial.

But back in the "good ole days" of the late 1800's, society was obsessed with putting an end to masturbation. Not only doctors, but also inventors committed themselves to stopping the perceived evil practice. The U.S. Patent Office sanctioned several anti-masturbation inventions during this period. From 1856 until 1917 at least twenty patents for such contraptions were issued.[42] The devices consisted of either sharp points that jabbed the erect penis or a small electrical shock administered when the young man was getting "out of control!" One apparatus patented in 1908 called "sexual armor" actually caged the penis so that its' movement was significantly limited. On the patent itself, the inventor, Ms Ellen Perkins, stated her reason for creating the device:

> *"It is a deplorable but well known fact that one of the most common causes of insanity, imbecility, and feeble mindedness, especially in youth, is due to masturbation or self-abuse. This is about equally true of both sexes."* [43]

Nutritionists of the era joined the anti-masturbation bandwagon with Dr. Sylvester Graham developing a special cracker that he said would control sexual urges and reduce tendencies to masturbate. What was this holy morsel? None other than the world-famous Graham Cracker![44]

Cereal developer John Kellogg also joined the crusade by developing his own cure to curb masturbation in children. What was his miracle masturbation missile? Believe it or not, Mr. Kellogg thought Cornflakes would certainly destroy the dark desire.[45] Cold cereal must not have been potent enough, however, for Mr. Kellogg needed more; history records that he received high powered enemas everyday in his rectum to supposedly keep him physically and sexually pure. Mr. Kellogg also bragged that he never made love to his wife and spent his honeymoon writing a book on the supposed evils of sex.[46] Others took up his sexophobic writing cause: Even as recently as the 20th century, books were still being written encouraging young people to stay away from spicy foods to curb their sexual temptations and masturbation urges.

To many of us in modern times this is laughable. But seriously, what is God's opinion about masturbation? That is the real issue for Christians. What does He have to say? The answer is surprising to some, but actually pretty clear: God has nothing to say about masturbation, absolutely nothing- not in the Bible, anyway. Some have referred to "Onan's sin" chronicled in Genesis 38 as "the sin of masturbation." The scripture in question says:

> *"Then Judah said to Onan, 'Lie with your brother's wife and fulfill your duty to her as a brother-in-law to produce offspring for your brother. But Onan knew that the offspring would not be his; so whenever he lay with his brother's wife, he spilled his semen on the ground to keep from producing offspring for his brother. What he did was wicked in the Lord's sight..." (Genesis 38:8-10a)*

The "wickedness" in Onan's behavior was that he did not fulfill his duty to provide offspring for his deceased brother. According to the custom of the time, and later commanded in the Law of Moses (Deut. 25:6), a man was obligated to have sex with his sister-in-law if his brother passed away without having a son. This carried on the family name and inheritance and legally gave the deceased man an heir. Onan, however, was angry that any son born would techni- cally not be considered his heir, but his brother's instead. To keep his deceased brother's wife from conceiving a child, Onan "spilled" his semen on the ground instead of allowing her to become impregnated with his "seed."

While this custom sounds foreign and crazy to most westerners living in the 21st century, it was extremely impor- tant in the ancient world where family, inheritance, and legacy meant everything.

Needless to say, this passage has absolutely nothing to do with masturbation. Onan wasn't masturbating and the passage was certainly not condemning the practice. Onan's sin was that he was not honoring his father or keeping the law of the land. He was disgracing his dead brother and his entire family. His heart was wicked and his actions selfish.

How this scripture came to be used to promote an anti-masturbation agenda is certainly bizarre. Masturbation was not being practiced or even considered in Genesis 38. Besides a few other references in the Law giving men and women instruction about how to "purify themselves" after emission of bodily fluids, sexual fluids, or blood-flow; nothing else is said in scripture that could be connected to masturbation.

Interestingly, much is said very specifically about other sexual practices, so the absence of instruction on this important subject is significant. Other writings from the ancient world did indeed discuss masturbation. It was obviously not a matter of ignorance. The Bible is simply silent on the issue.

What then should Christians do? Is masturbation acceptable for a Christ-centered, Spirit-filled believer? I suspect, like with many other issues, God desires that His people go beyond the "letter of the law" and look for His heart in the matter. (2 Corinthians 3:6) If by masturbating someone is damaging himself or herself by becoming obsessive or addictive; or if the practice is hurting a spouse by depriving him or her of conjugal rights or sexual pleasure, then it is wrong. Also, if masturbation is being used to fuel a sexual fantasy that the Holy Spirit has directed against, then it is wrong. On the other hand, if masturbation is being practiced by a single person who is trying to control their sexual passion by releasing sexual tension built up because of a commitment to abstinence or virginity, then it is not only ok, but probably a good strategy!

One of the things most precious to me when I married my wife was being able to present myself to her as a "virgin."

Not that I did not have opportunities growing up to be sexually active. I simply had a strong commitment to God and myself to wait until marriage to indulge in sexual intercourse. I believe that one of the reasons I was able to keep that commitment to God and myself was that I masturbated regularly during my dating years. Masturbating in my room away from women, thanking God for the wife He would one day give me, was far better than "losing it" on a date! I wasn't the only Christian young man who preserved himself in this way. In my Evangelical Christian college, one of our faculty dorm directors would counsel young men to masturbate in a private place accompanied by prayer and thanksgiving to God. This director was used powerfully to disciple young men and influence many of us to live radical, sold-out lives for Jesus.

Some of you can't believe what you are reading! You were always taught that masturbation was wrong. But remember our brief survey of church history and tradition regarding sexuality covered earlier in this book. A combination of Greek asceticism coupled with some of the early church fathers' anti-sex theological positions worked together to produce much confusion about these issues for many years throughout key formation periods of the church. The legacy of that confusion was a serious distortion of truth regarding human sexuality, including masturbation.

Whenever restrictive man-made rules (based on incorrect assumptions) become the teaching foundation of the church, there is a problem. Of the Pharisees, Jesus said:

"..their teachings are but rules taught by men."
(Mark 7:7)

Leaders should definitely be able to speak into the lives of the people that they shepherd. But when restrictive codes of conduct are implemented that potentially shackle God's people and unnecessarily hinder their freedom in Christ, then a problem arises. The Apostle Paul warned the Galatians;

> *"It is for freedom that Christ has set us free. Stand firm, then, and do not let yourselves be burdened again by a yoke of slavery." (Galatians 5:1)*

I'm sure this book is presenting a new perspective for many of you. But as I mentioned before, many Christians (throughout the years) have successfully used masturbation as a tool to stay chaste. Bestselling Christian author, Charlie Shedd in his book, **The Stork is Dead,** called masturbation a "gift from God" and suggested that it is a powerful tool to help singles avoid promiscuous sex.[47] Paul told the Thessalonians:

> *"It is God's will that you should be sanctified: that you should avoid sexual immorality; that each of you should learn to control his own body in a way that is holy and honorable..." (1 Thessalonians 4:3)*

Could it possibly be that one way for a hormonally-charged, sexually-alive Christian to "control the body" and "avoid immorality" is by a disciplined, Spirit-led walk that includes a periodic sexual release through masturbation? Masturbation makes it possible for unmarried singles who do not have the 'gift' of celibacy, to remain chaste. Instead of, "I've got to marry or I'll explode," masturbation buys time for single believers to seek God about the right choice for a mate. And for those who are married, masturbation provides a way to connect sexually to the thought of one another when family, career, or ministry responsibilities demand that time is spent apart. A man and his wife can fantasize about each other, masturbating while longing for each other when miles separate them from each another's arms. This pleasant exercise may actually strengthen the marriage, keeping thoughts of one another in the forefront of the mind and close to the heart. In such a case, masturbation is not merely a "solo act" but a reminder of love shared between people that are connected in covenant but separated by circumstance.

"But what about the single person's mindset?" someone asks, "Masturbation always involves sexual fantasy, so it must be wrong." Again, as we discussed in the last chapter, our understanding (or should I say misunderstanding) of sinful lust is clouding the issue. Sexual fantasy and sinful lust is not always the same thing. Biblically speaking, sinful lust is not merely a mental image or a dream date, but a heart decision, followed by corresponding action, to violate another human being and take what does not belong to me. Sinful lust is an issue of the heart, not the mind. The "lustful look" of Matthew 5:27-28 was wrong because it came out of a heart that had already decided to pursue a woman who was "off-limits." Again, in Jesus' Sermon on the Mount, it was a self-centered heart attitude plus an inappropriate action that followed which became "adultery of the heart."

If this is the case, then masturbation is not the same thing as sinful lust. Masturbation can indeed proceed from a heart that has already been adulterated and has already made a decision to compromise; but not everyone who masturbates has crossed that line and embraced sin. Masturbation can also be a guilt-free sexual release which helps preserve one's purity and sanity. Because of the biological and psychological release it provides, masturbation can actually help make a conscientious believer be *less* sexually oriented rather than more so in real-life relationships with people.

So instead of cornflakes, Graham crackers, penis pinchers, bland food, or electrical shock, I think my pastoral counsel regarding this subject of masturbation will continue to be "let the Spirit guide you." For people young and old, male and female, single and married, the key is to keep the heart pure and submitted to the will of God. Like many things in life, masturbation can either be a blessing or a curse, a tool or a snare, depending on the heart. Remember this brief, but powerful and revolutionary theological statement made by the Apostle Paul to his young disciple, Titus:

"To the pure, all things are pure, but to those who are corrupted and do not believe, nothing is pure..." (Titus 1:15)

Whether it is questions about fantasy, the thought life, sinful lust, or masturbation, one thing is certain – every Christian needs a healthy dose of discernment and self-control. Many things in life cannot simply be tagged "right" or "wrong." It depends on the context, the heart, the frequency, etc. Some things that are fine and even a blessing at one level can be harmful at another.

I often think of the bronze snake on the pole that God commanded Moses to erect in the desert. When anyone was bitten by a venomous snake, they were to look at that bronze snake and they would be healed. (Numbers 21:9) The snake was prophetic in that it prefigured Jesus Christ becoming the curse and hanging on the cross for the ultimate healing and salvation of mankind. (John 3:14) Unfortunately, the Israelites abused this prophetic tool and ended up worshipping the bronze snake years later. King Hezekiah, the reformer, correctly identified it as an idol and had it destroyed. (2 Kings 18:4) The very thing that God had given as a means of encountering his grace and power became a snare to the people when they misused it. The blessing turned into a curse. The object created by Moses to remind the people of God's faithfulness became an idol that took the place of God.

Many things in our earthly life like that bronze snake can become idols if we allow them: Experiences, sensations, hobbies, jobs, blessings, and even relationships - all legitimate things that God intends for us to enjoy and be blessed by, can actually become stumbling blocks if they are not under the Spirit's ultimate control.

God is the giver of all good gifts. His desire is to pour out all kinds of blessings on His children. (James 1:17) His gracious blessings are for us to enjoy (1 Timothy 6:17) and use to His glory. Our sexuality and even our sensuality are wonderful gifts from God. They are part of who we are as people. God has given us sensations, feelings, and even libido (sexual energy) that is to be celebrated, but always submitted to His purpose and plan. In appreciating and enjoying our sexuality, God will direct and lead us, revealing what behavior is appropriate for us and what is not.

Many times the difference between the two consists of being able to enjoy something to a point, but then being willing to lay it down or stop it at the appropriate time. Godly discipline teaches us to stop something before it turns into an obsession or addiction. Just like the bronze snake, a blessing can become a sinful burden if it is idolized. If you think about it, any human behavior, even neutral activities such as "surfing the net" or watching television, can become addictive if not kept in check.

The key to walking in victory is the age-old virtue of moderation or self-control. Self-control was the final "fruit of the Spirit" listed in Paul's description of the Spirit-led life in his message to the church in Galatia. (Galatians 5:22-23) The principle came up again as Paul exhorted his young protégé, Timothy. Challenging Timothy, he said:

> *"God did not give us a spirit of timidity, but a spirit of power, of love, and of **self-discipline**."*
> *(2 Tim. 1:7)*

In this verse, Paul was reminding Timothy of the reality of God's indwelling presence within the life of every believer. What an incredible promise God made to us, His people, that He would dwell within us through the promised Holy Spirit. Because of that indwelling, Paul encouraged young Christians saying:

> *"Christ in you, the hope of glory." (Colossians 1:27)*

This is the heart of Christianity: The wonderful fact that God not only accepts, but actually lives inside His people! The Holy Spirit brings to Christians the fullness of Christ. (Colossians 2:10) Because we are promised *fullness*, believers can expect both the character traits and the supernatural power of the risen Lord to be at work within our lives. The Spirit, then, not only leads believers, but also gives to them the resources of Christ's anointing. It is important to realize that self-control, the power to exercise restraint, comes from the indwelling Holy Spirit and not just from man's own natural resources. The power source is not the will of man, but the Spirit of God. Self-discipline or self-control is not just a good trait that some mature Christians possess: *It is the inheritance of every believer!*

The potential to walk in self-control lies within reach of every believer in Christ. It simply needs to be discovered and used. When the virtue of self-control is activated, we can properly experience life and enjoy it without becoming ensnared. Whenever anything "worldly" or sensory is enjoyed, we can savor the blessing of the moment without becoming a slave to it. Remember again Paul's word to the Galatians:

> *"It is for freedom that Christ has set us free..."*
> *(Gal. 5:1)*

Freedom without the leading and control of the Spirit can be a catastrophe. But freedom submitted to the authority of God makes life exciting, pleasurable, and filled with vitality. Again, consider Paul's description of the Spirit-filled life:

"For the kingdom of God is not a matter of eating and drinking but righteousness, peace, and joy in the Holy Spirit." (Romans 14:17)

God wants to get all of us into this place of freedom, victory, peace and joy. But to get there, it's essential that we work with the Holy Spirit and submit to His life-giving directives.

Self-control or self-discipline (called temperance or moderation in the older versions) is the mark of maturity that enables people to enjoy pleasures, even sexual ones, without being dominated or controlled by them. It's often the determining factor in figuring out whether something is right or wrong: Do I have control of the situation? Am I, and can I fully submit to God's will as I enjoy this activity?

Quite frankly, Christianity does not work well without self-control. No one can properly handle Christian freedom without this critical virtue. Self-control and self-discipline is what determines the difference between enjoying something and being addicted to it. Some ascetic types would rather throw out anything pleasurable or sensual, saying that it always corrupts. Actually, earthly pleasures and experiences do not always corrupt; but if Christians don't exercise proper self-restraint and discretion, they will.

Take, for instance, the issue of alcoholic beverages. Jesus clearly drank wine. His first recorded miracle was turning water into wine (John 2), and he was accused by the legalistic Pharisees of being a drunkard. (Luke 7:34) Jesus hung out with sinners (Mark 2:15-16), and he definitely drank wine at the table. Back then they knew, just as we know

now, that alcoholic beverages could be addictive and dangerous. Even the Old Testament Scriptures Jesus used contained warnings about wine. Consider this:

> *"Wine is a mocker and beer a brawler; whoever is led astray by them is not wise." (Proverbs 20:1)*

Using the arguments that many legalists and ascetics use today, Jesus was not wise to indulge in something that He knew by Scripture could be damaging. It was clear cut! No room for argument! But what about these *other* passages that come from the same Scriptures:

> *"...buy whatever you like...wine or other fermented drink, or anything else you wish. Then you and your household shall eat there in the presence of the Lord your God and rejoice." (Deuteronomy 14:26)*

Or this:

> *"Go, eat your food with gladness, and drink your wine with a joyful heart, for it is now that God favors what you do." (Ecclesiastes 9:7)*

And this:

> *"...new wine will drip from the mountains and flow from all the hills. I will bring back my exiled people...they will rebuild the ruined cities and live in them. They will plant vineyards and drink their wine..." (Amos 9: 13b-14a)*

Were the Scriptures sending out mixed messages? Was Jesus compromising by catering to the sensual desire for fine wine? Of course not! Jesus was in fact modeling the very virtue that is necessary to be fully sensual and completely spiritual at the same time. By sensual, I'm not implying that one behave in a sexually compromising manner or be controlled by the sinful nature. I do mean, however, that we emulate Jesus who was able to enjoy the pleasures of life without compromising his spiritual commitment or connection with God. He was able to discern the point where the simple pleasure ended and the possible addiction began. This line of discernment is discovered and respected by exercising His wisdom, listening for God, and using self-control. The same Holy Spirit that imparted wisdom, power, and self-control to Christ is available to do the same for us today. As believers we possess a treasure – the promised "Spirit of Christ" (Romans 8:9) living within us. Because of this treasure, we have access to supernatural resources. The Apostle Paul said:

> *"You...are not controlled by the sinful nature but by the Spirit, if the Spirit of God lives in you...And if the Spirit of him who raised Jesus from the dead is living in you, he who raised Christ from the dead will also give life to your mortal bodies through his Spirit, who lives in you." (Romans 8:9a, 11)*

The indwelling Spirit of God will bring "life" to our mortal bodies but deliver us from being controlled by them. The Spirit of God promises to bring grace, power, wisdom and genuine discernment to differentiate between innocent pleasures and sinful addiction.

Religious rule keeping often makes things overly simple – activities are either "good or bad," "sacred or secular," "black or white." But what about the grey? What about those things that can be either good or bad depending on the situation? Wine drinking, biblically, is one such issue – but there are many more. Alcohol consumption can be ok for some, even a blessing, but completely wrong for others. It can be right for someone in one circumstance, but completely wrong in another setting for the very same person. Many legalists do not like "the grey." I, for one, am learning to love it. For in the grey areas of uncertainty, I learn to pursue the heart of God. It's there that I discover how to hear His voice, capture His will, and discern His blessing and purpose for that special, unique moment in time. My spirituality then becomes relational, not merely religious. And it's in this place I learn to develop sensitivity to the Holy Spirit and self-control in my behavior.

Some, when they try to walk in the liberty of the Spirit, go crazy and abuse their freedom. Many times this occurs because they were raised with rigid rules and regulations. Even if their biological family was not like that, perhaps their church experience was. There was little need to exercise discernment or self-control in most activities; a thing was either wrong or right. When the former "teetotaler" is told he/she can have an occasional glass of wine, some "freak-out" with the new found freedom and drink too much. When a man is told he can appreciate a woman's beauty without being guilty of sinful lust, some guys go into "overload" and spend the next several weeks staring at women. These men have played the avoidance game so long; they act like adolescent boys when they are told its ok to look.

Yes, there is a danger in granting freedom; but there is also an incredible opportunity for growth. Every good parent knows this principle to be true. I would have never discovered the power and discipline of self-control if I was not first given my freedom. Remember again the words of Paul:

"It is for freedom that Christ has set us free. Stand firm, then, and do not let yourselves be burdened again by a yoke of slavery." (Galatians 5:1)

For Paul, it is because of this freedom that we can truly love others in a meaningful way:

"You, my brothers, were called to be free. But do not use your freedom to indulge the sinful nature; rather, serve one another in love. The entire law is summed up in a single command: Love your neighbor as yourself." (Galatians 5:13-14)

This freedom also takes us out of a system of law (rules and regulations) and gives us the opportunity of living by the constant leading of the Holy Spirit:

"So, I say, live by the Spirit, and you will not grat-ify the desires of the sinful nature...if you are led by the Spirit, you are not under law." (Galatians 5:16,18)

Because we are living in and by the Spirit, and walking in the love of God, our lives will produce good fruit which begin with love and end with self-control.

"But the fruit of the Spirit is love, joy, peace, patience, kindness, goodness, faithfulness, gentle-ness, and self-control. Against such things there is no law." (Galatians 5: 22-23)

The freedom of the Spirit does not make us a moral island unto ourselves. God has put checks and balances into place. There must be guidelines to protect us from deceiving ourselves. God has given us the faithful tool of Scripture.

The holy Scriptures are not supposed to be a blueprint for every situation, but a guidebook of principles that help us to discern the heart of God and the mind of Christ as we attempt to walk in the Spirit.

We have also been given the protective "covering" of godly authority. God has established His authority in the family, the church, and in civil government. He works through each one of these legitimate avenues of authority, guiding, directing, and protecting His people. To rebel against the human authority God has established is to rebel against Him, according to the Scriptures. (Romans 13:1-2) But under God's authority covering, there is still much room for each Christian to "wrestle with God," seek His will, and work out his/her own salvation. (Philippians 2:12) What is right for one may not be right for another; what is ok in one situation may be off-limits in another. (Romans 14) The Christian walk calls for a hearing ear and a yielded heart. It calls for discernment, discretion, and self-control. Praise God that self-control is not just the characteristic of the completely mature, but a fruit of the Spirit that can bloom on the youngest of trees!

CHAPTER 7

Questioning the Voice of Conscience

To properly understand Christian freedoms, liberties, and responsibilities, it is essential to consider the often neglected subject of "the conscience." Christian freedom cannot be exercised in faith if the believer is not walking in step with his/her conscience. Conscience is referred to over and over again in the Scriptures, but not discussed much in modern day Christian circles. What really is the conscience? Theologians have debated that question for centuries.

The concept of conscience actually came from the Greeks whose philosophers greatly influenced society before, during, and after the life of the Apostle Paul. Paul would often use their terminology in expressing the truths of the gospel. The basic Greek word for conscience is *"syneidenai"* which means "knowing oneself; or to bear inner witness to one's own conduct in a moral sense." [48]

Famous Greek philosophers like Cicero and Seneca interpreted the word as "the trial of oneself, sometimes in accusation, sometimes in defense."[49] Paul believed that even pagan Gentiles in the nations who were truth seekers had this built in moral compass. To the Romans he said:

> *"Indeed when Gentiles, who do not have the law, do by nature things required by the law, they are a law for themselves, even though they do not have the law, since they show that the requirements of the law are written on their hearts, their consciences also bearing witness, and their thoughts now accusing, now even defending them." (Romans 2:14-15)*

This "moral compass" or conscience is part of what makes us uniquely human and differentiates us from the animal kingdom. It is obviously not unique to believers in Jesus, but universal to all people. The conscience is a precious gift God has given mankind which should not be violated, an inner voice which must be heard. For the Apostle Paul, everyone who is seeking God has a responsibility to follow the leading of their conscience.

Many areas of morality are clear in regard to what is right and wrong. But some things are not quite so simple. One such area, in the early church, was the issue of food sacrificed to idols. To get good, inexpensive (and sometimes free) meat, Christians had to pick and chose from meat that had been involved in ritual sacrifice to pagan deities. Was it right or wrong to eat meat that had been "tainted" in this way? Paul believed it was ok if the believer prayed over the food and dedicated it to God. (1 Tim 4:3-5) However, if another person was in the room who had a problem of conscious regarding the eating of the meat, the believer should refrain. The way Paul saw it, if a person had a "weak conscious" and could not eat with confidence, he/she could actually be damaged by indulging in food that had been used in an idol sacrifice, (1 Corinthians 8:11-13) since the eating of such food would be done in fear and not by faith.

(Romans 14:23)

Therefore, the issue is not just, "What does God say," or even, "What does the Christian leader say," but also, "What does my conscience say?" Something can be "theologically ok" but wrong for me if I can not do it by faith, or with good conscience. Speaking of ritual purity concerns about food, Paul told the Romans:

> *"As one who is in the Lord Jesus, I am fully convinced that no food is unclean in itself." (Rom 14:14a)*

Even though that truth had been firmly established in Paul's heart, he went on to say:

> *"...But if anyone regards something as unclean, then for him it is unclean." (Rom 14:14b)*

In other words, even if God says something is ok for one person, if another person has a *conscientious* problem with it, for that person the activity is wrong. The inner voice of the conscious becomes important, therefore, in determining what behavior is appropriate, and what is not. Paul repeats the principle a few verses later making the point even stronger by saying:

> *"But the man who has doubts is condemned if he eats, because his eating is not from faith; and everything that does not come from faith is sin." (Roman 14:23)*

Conscious determines to a certain degree what is sin for me. On the one hand, my freedom should not be stymied by someone else's moral view, but on the other hand, someone else's liberty does not make the activity right for me.

Conservative Christians love absolute truth. Many of us love for things to be either clearly right or absolutely wrong. It is much simpler when things are "black or white" as opposed to gray. Christian morality, however, is just not always that easy. What love (for God, others, and self) requires in one instance is not necessarily what it requires in another.

Believers must be sensitive to the Spirit of God and to their own consciences to determine what behavior is right for them. However, as we will see later, the conscience's perception of truth is not always accurate, and it is frequently changing and growing as it receives new input or information. Individual consciences may lead different directions in different people. Sometimes a person's conscience may lead one way in one situation, but another way in a different circumstance. This makes some ethical decisions *situational* as opposed to absolute. Again, not every thing we look at in our Christian experience comes to us as "black or white" but many issues are gray. These "gray areas" of Christian morality force believers to "wrestle" with God and pursue Him to determine the best course of action. This pursuit of God is good because it takes us out of the culture of mere "religion" and into the realm of relationship with God.

Christianity, in its pure form, is a relationship-based, experiential religion. Rules and regulations are not adequate. Believers are drawn into a new matrix of communication with God through the Holy Spirit. This means that I cannot simply adopt the morality of another believer, I must find my own. Neither should I judge another believer based on my view of what is holy, I must allow them to pursue their own direction from God.

This is not to say that there are no absolutes. There certainly are! But there are many gray areas that demand that we pursue God on our own and extend grace to others to do the same. Speaking of these "gray" areas, Paul said:

"Accept him whose faith is weak, without passing judgment on disputable matters. One man's faith allows him to eat everything, but another man, whose faith is weak, eats only vegetables. The man who eats everything must not look down on him who does not, and the man who does not eat everything must not condemn the man who does, for God has accepted him. Who are you to judge someone else's servant?...One man considers one day more sacred than another; another man considers every day alike. Each one should be fully convinced in his own mind...You then, why do you judge your brother? Therefore let us stop passing judgment on one another. (Romans 14:1-4a, 5,10a, 13a)

My own conscious, *is* critical in determining what is right or wrong behavior for me. I cannot judge another, but I must be consistent and true to my own beliefs. The conscience serves as my inner moral judge.

The Scriptures are clear, however, that my conscience can become "corrupted" through guilt, sin, idolatry, or even legalism. (1 Timothy 4:2-5; Titus 1:15) When tainted, the conscience can be used by the enemy to bring confusion and distort the truth. On one extreme, a corrupted conscience can rationalize sin; on the other, it can torment people with undue guilt – telling them things are sinful that really are not. When contemporary Bible teachers and preachers speak of a "corrupt conscious," they are often talking about the hardening of the conscience that comes as a result of sin or rebellion against God. It is true that habitual sin has a way of "deadening" the conscience's voice of moral protest against damaging, selfish behavior.

But the conscience can also be corrupted in the opposite way. It can be influenced by legalism, polluted to the point where it actually works against the truth, deafening people to the authentic, life-giving words of God. Paul warned Timothy about so-called teachers who would come in and put people into legalistic bondage through their false teachings. Consider this warning:

> *"The Spirit clearly says that in later times some will abandon the faith and follow deceiving spirits, and things taught by demons. Such teachings come through hypocritical liars, **whose consciences have been seared as with a hot iron.** (Emphasis mine). They forbid people to marry and order them to abstain from certain foods, which God created to be received with thanksgiving by those who believe and who know the truth. For everything God created is good, and nothing is to be rejected if it is received with thanksgiving, because it is consecrated by the word of God and prayer." (1 Timothy 4:1-5)*

Notice that their conscience had been "seared" in a legalistic way. These false teachers were calling things "sin" that God calls "good." They were feeling convicted for things that were not really sinful at all. And even worse, they were putting those burdens on others as well. This is the "yeast of the Pharisees" that Jesus warned about. (Matthew 16:6) He strongly rebuked the legalistic Pharisees for the way that their teachings were pushing people away rather than drawing them near to God. Jesus said:

> *"And you experts in the law, woe to you, because you load people down with burdens they can hardly carry, and you yourselves will not lift one finger to help them." (Luke 11:46)*

Today there are voices in the church world that major in putting God's people down. They constantly blast the church and society as a whole in the Name of Jesus. Instead of being known for love (John 13:35), they become known instead for their apparent hatred for humanity. Although they use Scriptures, their messages carry more death than life. Even the legalistic Pharisees knew the Scriptures extremely well, but they missed the point, and missed the Messiah when He was standing right in front of them. Jesus said about them:

> *"You diligently study the Scriptures because you think that by them you possess eternal life. These are the Scriptures that testify about me, yet you refuse to come to me to have life." (John 5:39-40)*

They knew the Scriptures, but they did not have the heart or true revelation of God. Even if they were following their consciences, their consciences were terribly misinformed. They had the "letter of the law" but not the Spirit. (2 Corinthians 3:6) Unfortunately, this "tribe" is still with us today. Instead of perceiving how powerfully God is moving in the world today, awakening people to a new level of spiritual hunger and passion for God, these modern Pharisees instead seem to only see sin and judgment.

And just like the original Pharisees criticized and opposed the ministry of Jesus, these modern day legalists ignore or condemn the fresh winds of the Spirit of God being breathed out upon the people of the world. Some of them even put down believers and churches who are involved in Holy Spirit renewal. These critical spirits have labeled some of what God is graciously pouring forth as "false or counterfeit revival." I am one who is a witness both in the United States and around the world that the rivers of revival are legitimate and God is doing a new and glorious thing. (Isaiah 43:19)

I am, however, also very concerned about a "false revival." Not the legitimate movement or manifestation of the Spirit; but a "false revival" that seems to occur when God's people are made to feel guilty and unworthy. In revival services like these, Christians are often mercilessly criticized by preachers who focus on their failures. People are "encouraged" (sometimes manipulated) to come to an altar to repent for their desperate condition and receive a blessing of prayer promised to absolve their guilty hearts of a terrible, backsliding, sinful condition (until next week's service!). The "move of God" in this type of meeting is often measured by the number of people at the altar and the amount of tears in their eyes.

Certainly, God does use conviction, and many people need to repent. We have had some beautiful meetings where people were laying prostrate before God and tears were freely flowing. But some modern Pharisees do not see the Kingdom of God beyond the weeping altar. The weeping altar becomes the goal of every meeting. Some of these preachers are actually blind to the image of God in people because they are focusing exclusively on the sinful nature. They have learned "old-time religion" and habitually put God's people down, making them feel that they will never be holy enough to receive any real blessing or breakthrough in their lives.

Again, God IS into repentance, and one should at times have a broken and contrite heart before the Lord. But when this kind of meeting and this kind of spirit dominates believers' Christian experience, they will never move ahead into the grace-based, Christ-conscious place of joy, peace, and victory that God has ordained. Grief over sin must be replaced at some point by confidence in the finished work of Calvary. People need to move beyond sin consciousness into Christ-consciousness where the terror of God is replaced by love for the Father, and boldness to enter with joy into His presence. (Hebrews10:19-22) Just as I am concerned about "feeding the sinful flesh" through undisciplined eroticism, I am just as concerned about feeding a "seared, legalistic conscience" through fear based, sin-centered preaching.

I fear that many precious believers throughout the body of Christ have consciences "seared through legalism" that have become more useful at this point to Satan, the "accuser of the brethren" (Rev 12:11) than they are to the Spirit of God. Remember the conscience can be a wonderful tool of the Spirit, but it can also be a weapon of the enemy if it has been corrupted.

The conscious is a useful guide, but not an infallible one. It serves as an inner moral judge who must be obeyed if we are to remain true to ourselves. This inner "judge," however, can be misinformed and need new information and revelation to serve us more effectively. Recognizing both the value and potential limitation or distortion of our conscience's perspective will help us be able to reevaluate some old opinions based on new revelation and insight. In discussing the conscience, world- renowned theologian, Paul Tillich, had this to say about its reliability:

> "...the conscience witnesses to the law (either the Mosaic or natural law), but it does not contain the law. Therefore, its judgment can be wrong. Paul speaks of a "weak conscience" when describing the narrow and timid attitude of Christians who are afraid to buy meat in the market because it might have been used in pagan cults. Paul criticizes such attitudes. But he emphasizes that even an erring conscience must be obeyed. And he warns those who are strong in conscience not to induce, by their example, those who are weak to do things that would give them an uneasy conscience."[50]

Properly understanding the conscience and how it works is critical for discerning the will of God and the "voice of God" for our lives. Speaking as a pastor who leads a nondenominational church within the "charismatic" portion of the larger body of Christ, I frequently hear people refer to their own discernment as the voice of God. "God told me this, or God told me that" is common within the church circles I serve. As much as I believe in the necessity of Christians hearing the "voice of God" (John 10, 1 Corinthians 2), I also believe we should learn to distinguish between God's voice and our own conscience. I suspect that much of what has been attributed to the voice of God is actually the voice of inner conscience. Separating the two might be an inexact science, but certainly is a necessary one.

The voice of conscience can and should change its opinion as we grow. God, on the other hand, , while He may change His specific strategy for His child's life based on changing circumstances or situations, will never alter His view of truth. When we get conscience and God's specific revelation mixed up together; that is, when for us the voice of conscience and the voice of God is one and the same, we potentially create a great deal of confusion for ourselves. Actually, we can end up significantly hindering our growth in Christ when we fail to make this critical distinction.

For instance, a sensitive Christian man may make a bold claim related to his sexuality such as "God told me that when I looked at that woman I lusted." Or, a young lady when told she looks gorgeous in what she is wearing might confess, "Thank you. I like it too, but God convicted me that the outfit was sinful and I should never wear it again." Let's say, for the sake of argument, that in each of these cases the believers in question were not actually responding to God's voice, but to their own consciences. With new information and revelation the man realizes that what he thought was sinful lust was actually just normal male sexual awareness and drive. The young lady also changes her mind because she realizes that her view of modesty was based more in her conservative fundamental Christian upbringing than it was on the Word of God or the leading of the Holy Spirit. Though the outfit complements her and "accentuates the positives," it is not overly distracting to others or causing them to stumble. So in both cases as these two believers change their minds about God's perspective, the "voice of their conscience" changes its' tune as well. If the man had said at first, "I feel like I lusted," or the girl, "I feel this outfit is inappropriate," then it would have been less confusing and more consistent when they then later changed their opinion after praying over new input and receiving a fresh perspective on God's truth.

The point to be made is that we would serve ourselves and others better if we would adopt the "language of conscience" instead of tagging the Name of the Lord to every opinion we hold. To say, "I feel this way or that way," is more honest, and reveals a proper understanding of the role conscience plays in our understanding of things. I say this in no way to diminish the fact that believers can and desperately need to hear God speak as well. But through discovering, understanding, and even analyzing the conscience — its strengths as well as its limitations — we will be able to more accurately discern God's voice when He does have something specific to say.

Another situation that demands believers consider the issues of conscience is when a particular behavior or activity could potentially injure someone else. Individual Christian freedom must always bow to the principle of serving one another and building up one another. Paul says:

> *"Everything is permissible – but not everything is beneficial. Everything is permissible – but not*

everything is constructive. Nobody should seek his own good, but the good of others." (1Corinthians 10:23-24)

Later in the same chapter the apostle gives an illustration of this principle at work. The specifics of the situation may seem foreign to us, but the underlying principles speak loudly and clearly teaching us the boundaries of our freedom in Christ.

The issue was whether or not to eat meat which had been used in animal sacrifice to pagan gods. Paul had just warned the young believers that such sacrifices were off-limits to Christians, and could actually put believers in contact with demonic powers (1 Corinthians 10:19-22). But, as mentioned before, the practical problem was that much of the meat available in the markets came from such sacrifices. Was it ok to go ahead and eat that meat as long as you were not participating in the actual pagan worship service? This was a "red hot" question at the time, the answer to which affected most everybody in the church at Corinth that Paul was overseeing. His solution was that the believers who could handle eating such meat without feeling that they had compromised could go ahead and do so privately. But if a Christian was invited to someone else's home who made a big deal out of the fact that the meat had been used in pagan worship, then the Christian should not eat it "for conscience sake," Paul adds, "the other man's conscience, I mean, not yours." (1 Corinthians 10:29) In other words, the Christian should be sensitive to both his/her own conscience and the consciences of others involved in a shared activity.

A modern day illustration follows: Several years ago my wife was "out on the town" with some Christian women who were having a good time together. In a restaurant, one of the ladies suggested they enjoy margaritas together. My wife abstained, but several of the women ordered the alcoholic drink. When she got home that evening, my wife Sheila was very frustrated because one of the women in the group was a new believer who had come out of a desperate, alcoholic past. She was probably not ready to be exposed to the scenario forced upon her that night. The other Christian ladies should have been more discerning, more sensitive to her struggle, but were not. Though it might have been appropriate in another situation, drinking the alcoholic beverages was inappropriate and wrong on this particular occasion. As Paul was saying, it was wrong "for conscience sake – the other person's conscience." (1 Corinthians 10:28-29)

Conscience must be considered when determining whether or not something is right or wrong. In private matters, it is simply a matter of looking into your own conscience to either "bear witness to" or reject the activity in question. In public matters, however, the consciences of others must be considered as well. This implies that Christians must engage in genuine, honest, open conversations about moral issues with one another. In these situations, however, we must understand that what is morally right for one may not be for another. The key is to honor God, be faithful to our own conscience, and sensitive one to another.

What is the conclusion of the matter, then, as it relates to our freedom and conscience? The Biblical reply would go something like this: Live connected to and led by the Spirit of God; be submitted to godly authority: live true to your own conscience, and do everything in love. But as you listen for the inner voice, be ready to grow and change as God continues to heal your conscience, enrich your understanding, and direct your steps. Rejoice that God has given you both a sensitivity to and freedom of conscience. Paul said:

"...why should my freedom be judged by another's conscience? If I take part in the meal with thankfulness, why am I denounced because of

something I thank God for? So whether you eat or drink or whatever you do, do it all for the glory of God. Do not cause anyone to stumble...even as I try to please everybody in every way. For I am not seeking my own good but the good of many so that they may be saved." (1 Corinthians 10:32-33)

CHAPTER 8

Light Shining in Dark Places

I'll never forget the setting: It was Sunday night after church and the youth group was having a discussion in the local Pizza parlor. The issue at hand was dancing. Could a Christian dance; should a Christian dance? My parents said I could make the decision on my own, but my mind was already made up. To me, as a conscientious (but somewhat legalistic) Christian young man the answer seemed clear: I could not go to the dance. For that matter, I should not dance anytime or anywhere. I knew myself. Like every other young man I knew, I struggled with raging hormones. My thinking was simple and clear-cut: How could I hold a young lady next to me without being sexually aroused, at least to some degree? And since I associated all sexual arousal with lust, then the obvious answer was, "No – I could not dance."

Because of this decision (and others like it), I separated myself somewhat from the culture of my High School. My sophomore year a senior girl asked me to the prom. She was a precious girl – kind, fun loving, and popular. But I had to turn her down and say no. Seeing a disappointed and per-plexed look in her eyes, I tried in vain to explain why I couldn't go to the dance.

I was a popular kid in my Junior High and High School days (mainly with other Christian young people), but often felt as if I were on the outside looking in at the world going on around me. I had a deep love for God and my heart burned to see people's lives genuinely transformed by His love and power. I desired to lead my friends to Christ and even had a measure of success. Now I am certain, without a doubt, that I could have been much more effective in taking Jesus into my world if I would have been more involved in the lives and activities of my non-Christian friends. I often think back, wondering if I had been free then from some of the legalistic views I was famous for, how much more significantly could I have impacted that school for God?

Jesus was controversial. He went to the "dances." He hung out with the sinners. He was a welcome guest at parties and enjoyed good food. As a matter of fact, his very first recorded miracle was changing water into wine at a wedding party where the folks had certainly enjoyed plenty to drink. And this was not just *any* wine he served, mind you, but very fine wine! The guests bragged about its superior taste. (John 2:1-11)

The religious legalists of the time did not approve of Jesus' fraternization with the lost. They thought he was compromising. Speaking of the Pharisees distaste for his approach to ministry, Jesus said:

> *"The Son of Man came eating and drinking, and they say, 'Here is a glutton and a drunkard, a friend of tax collectors and sinners." (Matthew 11:19)*

Jesus did not seem to be overly concerned about being corrupted or polluted by his associations with the lost. He even spent time with prostitutes! Jesus' conviction was that it wasn't external contact with the world that made people unclean, but only what came out of their hearts. Listen again to his words from the book of Mark:

> *"Listen to me, everyone, and understand this. Nothing outside a man can make him unclean by going into him. Rather, it is what comes out of a man that makes him unclean."* (Mark 7:14-15)

Many Christians have felt the need to insulate themselves from the world. The problem with this kind of thinking is that it makes it virtually impossible to radically impact society with the gospel if we have nothing to do with it. As believers we *are* to separate ourselves from a sinful, selfish mindset that's in the world, *but not from its people*. When God uses us to touch someone or impact a life for Christ, we need not worry that their sin habits will automatically contaminate us. Some Christians avoid worldly people as if they were carrying a contagious disease that could be caught like the common cold! Not to worry, the Spirit of God protects the believer. Consider the Lord's awesome promise to his people:

> *"I have given you authority...to overcome all the power of the enemy; nothing will harm you."* (Luke 10:19)

The Apostle John reminded his followers of the same fact:

> *"...the one who is in you is greater than the one who is in the world."* (1 John 4:4)

John is well-known for his saying, "Do not love the world or anything in the world..." (1 John 2:15). To properly understand this, however, it is important to realize that he was talking about that which belonged to and originated from the sinful nature or flesh of man. He was not speaking about simple pleasures, but fleshly pride, greed, and covetousness. Like the Apostle Paul, John believed Christians should expect to experience victory over the sinful nature and be liberated into a whole new kind of victorious existence.

John taught that believers don't have to wait for heaven to experience eternal life, but that eternal life is a present reality for those who walk with God. His desire for believers was

> *"That you may **know** that you have eternal life."*
> *(1 John. 5:13)*

According to both Jesus and his apostles, believers should not have to run and hide from the world, even from its brokenness and sin. Empowered by the Spirit, followers of Jesus Christ must impact the world with God's power and love and change it. Jesus told his disciples:

> *"You are the light of the world. A city on a hill cannot be hidden. Neither do people light a lamp and put it under a bowl. Instead they put it on its stand, and it gives light to everyone in the house. In the same way, let your light shine before men, that they may see your good deeds and praise your Father in heaven. (Matthew 5:14-16)*

God's cutting edge strategy for the church is not that we retreat from the world, but transform it instead by spreading His flame of love to broken humanity. The world doesn't need believers to simply point out its' brokenness and sin, but to reveal the heart of God. The Lord has not called us to run from the darkness, but to illuminate it with the light of

His Presence. Thankfully, we will not absorb darkness just because we come into contact with it. On the contrary we overcome it! Light is always stronger than darkness. Our light is not meant to be hidden under a bowl, but to be on display for the world to see and appreciate!

Regarding sexual stimuli, believers need to realize that we will constantly come into contact with movies, pictures, and people that do not represent God's highest standards of sexual purity. Consider Jesus with the Samaritan woman at the well. (John 4) He could have condemned her. The poor lady had already been married five times, and the man she had at the moment was not her husband. But instead of lecturing her on sexual sin, Jesus chose to offer her a drink of living water. His conversation with her did not make light of her sexual brokenness, but lifted her instead into a place of hope. After this brief encounter with the Master, the woman became the chief spokesperson for the Kingdom of God in her town, excitedly sharing about Jesus with others and leading them out to meet him.

Our approach to the world should be patterned after this incredible example. Instead of condemning those around us with sexual brokenness, we should share with them living water. And rather than condemning ourselves for being sexually stimulated to some degree by alluring images, we should rejoice that God has our heart. Because Jesus is Lord and living within us, we will not compromise our standards. Being exposed to sexual images or thoughts does not have to change my values or behavior. Though an arousing image may fly across my line of sight or invade my thoughts or dreams, by God's power I chose not to act upon that thought or image in any way whatsoever.

Adultery of the heart does not occur unless I act in some way upon a heart decision to compromise my standards or someone else's. As we have discovered through a careful study of God's Word, it is ungodly flirtation or conscious pursuit of someone who is "off-limits" that Jesus condemns as coming from a wicked heart.

Being exposed to that which is overly sensual or even sinful may not always be easy, but it does not have to be deadly. Many Christians, however, move in such fear that they are paralyzed by this kind of contact with the world. The result is that they become completely defensive instead of offensive. Instead of seeing hurting people and crying out to God for strategy to impact them with His love, many traditional believers are running away from what scares them. The enemy is rendering many virtually helpless through this kind of intimidation.

If the devil can't take your salvation away, he will do his best to immobilize you and keep you ineffective in the Kingdom of God. That way, though he has lost you, he won't lose many others because of you. Being "afraid of the dark" has kept many Christians from changing the world. It's about time that we quit running away with fear and become confident in His power to keep us holy. Remember these powerful words from Jude:

> *To Him who is able to keep you from falling and to present you before his glorious presence without fault and with great joy – to the only God our Savior be glory, majesty, power and authority, through Jesus Christ our Lord, before all ages, now and forevermore! Amen (Jude 24-25)*

It's time that we become comfortable with the fact that we are both sexual and spiritual people. Although exposed to and tempted by sexual sin, we choose not to compromise. That is, we choose not to *act upon* any image or thought that would compromise our commitment to God, hurt ourselves or damage someone else. With this newfound confidence, we will remain undisturbed by the enemy's futile attempt to capitalize on our sexual vulnerabilities.

In the late 90's a sci-fi movie called *The Matrix* quickly became a favorite to fans of that genre. In the movie, the lead character came to realize that his world was not real, but only a computer induced reality being fed into his mind through a mega-computer. When he finally escaped this "false reality," the hero and a group of renegade freedom fighters hooked themselves back up to the computer in a unique way and went into "the matrix" to rescue people from its power. The enemy "agents" were also in the matrix, hunting down the freedom fighters.

If the heroes were hit by gunfire, even though they were in this false world called "the matrix," they still could die. The lead character learned to avoid the enemy's bullets through highly developed martial arts skills. Then, in a final showdown at the end of the movie, the hero finally discovered that he didn't need to avoid the bullets any longer. He had power over them. For in reality, he existed at a higher level than the bullets, and if he understood and meditated upon that fact, the power of his faith would nullify any effect the bullets could have on him.

A generation earlier, this same theme was used (albeit in simpler form) in another sci-fi classic – the television series, *Star Trek*. In one famous episode the crew of the starship Enterprise was visiting a planet that seemed to be a re-creation of the old west with literal characters from American history running around playing their parts. Old-West Sheriff Wyatt Earp was there tracking down the Enterprise crew who he thought were famous outlaws.

Finally, in the last scene, the Enterprise crew realized the whole scenario was an alien mind game of some kind. The upcoming gun battle, no matter how real it seemed could not be real. As long as they believed the "truth" and did not fear the bullets, the gunshots could not hurt them at all. So

Spock, the famous Vulcan scientist from the Enterprise crew, convinced the rest of his mates to face the gun battle with confidence, assurance, and mental resolve. They did, and the bullets flew by them without effect.

Although these stories are just fictional tales, they have parabolic value to illustrate the truth about the lives of Kingdom people as Jesus and His disciples understood it. The Lord was (and still is) calling forth a "chosen people" who will be free from the guilt and power of sin. Though they live *in* the world, they are not *of* this world. In other words, they can touch the fallenness of humanity without absorbing it into their hearts.

The bullets, if you will, don't have to lodge in our souls! In the sexual realm, Jesus is calling us as his people to be strong enough and secure enough in grace to face various sexual stimuli and even temptation without compromising our convictions.

Many Christians believe it is impossible for an honest believer to live in Hollywood and be an actor. "There's too much sexual temptation, too much compromise," they say. Thinking like that is unfortunate and narrow-minded. God wants to "plant" believers in strategic places that will impact the planet. I can't think of any position more strategic in the modern world than one who is successful as an actor. Well-known actors are some of the most influential people on the globe; they are also some of the wealthiest. It's time for the power of wealth and influence to come into the hands of the righteous that will use it to the glory of God! His Kingdom will eventually invade all the kingdoms of this world. How much that holy Kingdom advances in our day is largely dependant on our level of expectation, faith, and availability. We are his body, and we are the ones who will yield to the Spirit and allow God to lead us into strategic places. How big is our vision? Or, better stated, how big is our God? Will He find any faith to work with? Are there any "out of the box" believers out there ready to go after the enemy's territory? I believe there are. The ones the Lord will send into Hollywood will not be out-of-touch, uptight, "scared of the dark" legalists. No, the ones He sends will have huge hearts for people, confidence in God's keeping power, and a joy and freedom in Christ that makes the world stand up and take notice! "What is it you have?" they will ask; "something about you is different." God is looking for regular people, "jars of clay," to carry forth and demonstrate His treasure. He is looking for incarnation: Kingdom people that can "become flesh and dwell among" the people of the world.

Unfortunately, many believers are focused on escape – hiding out, avoiding the world, and waiting for the rapture. Unfortunately, this mentality will never really accomplish the goal of transforming culture with the Gospel of the Kingdom. Throughout church history, many precious believers have become miserable people and terrible testimonies of God's grace and power because of their obsession with escaping evil. Instead of being bridge-builders looking to connect regular people with the God who died for them, many legalists have neglected the very people they were commissioned to save because they're afraid of "getting dirty."

Our responsibility to impact the world obviously does not give us as believers license to "play with the dirt." We have not been set free from the guilt and power of sin only to go back and wallow in it! Freedom does not mean we indulge in sinful behavior or do whatever our heart (or flesh) desires! Some of the Corinthians misunderstood Paul's message of grace as a carte blanche endorsement of hedonism – the unrestricted pursuit of pleasure. While maintaining the truth of their freedom in Christ, Paul checked their undisciplined outlook saying:

> *"Everything is permissible for me – but not every-*

thing is beneficial. Everything is permissible for me – but I will not be mastered by anything." (1 Corinthians 6:12)

The Apostle Paul was challenging believers to use the "mind of Christ" (1 Corinthians 2:16) that had been given to them, praying and thinking through their behavior to insure that their lifestyle was building other's up and bringing glory to God. He further exhorted them to make a decision not to be "mastered by anything," (1 Corinthians 6:12) except, of course, by the Spirit of God.

For us today, the challenge is the same. Although I have liberty to enjoy earthly pleasures, they must not be allowed to control or govern my life. If at any point some earthly pleasure or pursuit keeps me from hearing and obeying God, it becomes an idol to me. Idolatry is always sinful. What psychologists often call addiction, the Spirit of God calls idolatry. Not every thing that leads to addiction or idolatry is necessarily bad in itself. Even neutral or good things can become wrong if they take charge of my life.

According to the Scriptures, Christians should not let anything else in life control them but the Spirit of God. Every decision and action should be analyzed and evaluated by Christ's Law of love. The Spirit of God is in charge. The Lord is leading us, not the sinful nature. Even legitimate desires of the body or soul should not be allowed to direct our lives.

This is not bad news, but good news! Being delivered from sensual control actually allows me to enjoy sensual pleasures even more! If I become enslaved to something, it loses its appeal and becomes utterly destructive. Many drug addicts can attest that what once began with a "feel-good high" disintegrates into a necessary fix that brings more despair than real pleasure. Only when earthly pleasures are submitted to God's original design and purpose can they really be a continual source of blessing and joy. When enjoyed in the right context, the pleasures of life should be a source of praise for the believer. According to Scripture, bodily pleasures, emotional fulfillment, and all earthly blessings are to be received with thanksgiving as long as these temporal things do not control our lives. To his young protégé Timothy, Paul wrote these words:

> *"For everything God created is good, and nothing is to be rejected if it is received with thanksgiving, because it is consecrated by the word of God and prayer." (1 Timothy 4:4-5)*

> *"...hope in God, who richly provides everything for our enjoyment." (1 Timothy 6:17b)*

And to the church in Colossae, he said:

> *"And whatever you do, whether in word or deed, do it all in the name of the Lord Jesus, giving thanks to God the Father through him." (Colossians 3:17)*

The Apostle Paul was certainly not "anti-body" or "anti-pleasure" as were later Christian theologians who followed him. Paul believed Christians should thoroughly enjoy life and make the most of it. He even described God's Kingdom as it intersects the life of the believer as "righteousness, peace, and joy in the Holy Spirit." (Romans 14:14)

The real secret to loving God completely, enjoying life fully, and walking in total victory is to learn to continually keep all things in a proper "Kingdom of God" perspective. As a famous missionary once said, "We must live our lives in the shadow of eternity." Earthly life is to be treasured and enjoyed, but it is not the final destination. We must be constantly aware of and sensitive to the eternal consequences of our attitudes and actions. This is what the Apostle Peter meant when he said believers were to live "as aliens and strangers in the world." (1 Peter 2:11). It is not that we can't enjoy life, but we must realize that our real goals and values are eternal and transcend this earthbound existence.

A wasted life, in effect, is one that does not consider eternity or make an eternal difference in the lives of others. But when life is enjoyed with an eternal sensitivity and perspective, the glory of God's Kingdom – His wonderful Presence and incredible promises – radiate from us and through us to others *even in this life!*

To walk in this glorious connection with God, He calls on us to evaluate the motives of our hearts and consider the effects of our actions on the lives of others. This is a life of tremendous freedom but also of great responsibility. It's not a mystical walk of faith measured through nebulous spiritual thoughts, but a practical Christianity that displays its worth in loving ministry to God and to others. It is not a treasure the devil can steal through a fleeting thought or temptation; but it's a protected place connected to God who will continue to keep us as we seek first His Kingdom.

What God really wants for us as His people is that we would know Him personally and live victoriously. We are destined to live free from the power of guilt and sin, full of joy and peace, and overflowing with His awesome love.

God has promised to protect our hearts through the seal of His Holy Spirit. By His grace we can and will live guilt-free, grace-filled, Spirit-directed lives. We won't "fear the bullets" but be confident in the protective power of God. We will enjoy life fully, with all its wonderful sensations and pleasures, but at the same time, live radically for Him. Our task is not to deny pleasure, or be ashamed of it, but to redeem all the blessings of life for God's holy, loving purposes.

As an integral part of who we are, our sexuality is a critical part of our human existence that should be embraced and enjoyed to the glory of God. We are not to compromise our convictions, our conscience, or the principles of Scripture. Neither are we to punish ourselves for being sexual, feeling sexual, or appreciating the genuine sexuality of those around us.

This world is a wonderfully sensual place! It is filled with flowers, all kinds of flowers. The earth is really in fact, a work of art, beautifully designed by a master artist: He carefully planned his masterpiece, making it beautiful and wonderful with man, His ultimate creation, at the center of it all. As part of their human experience, the Creator blesses His children with views, scents, tastes, colors, smells, sensations, sounds, songs, emotions, dreams, desires, and of course, other people! Fully experiencing these things is all part of what it means to be human. Can we be fully sensual and fully spiritual at the same time? Is it ok to really enjoy life? Can we appreciate the beauty, possessions, and company of others without coveting them and lusting after something that we cannot or should not have? Can we walk through someone else's garden, smell a flower, and enjoy its scent without having to pluck it and possess it? I think the answer to all these questions is a resounding "yes!"

I also know that God is calling forth a people who can redeem what it means to thrive as God-connected humans: living fully, laughing heartily, feeling deeply, serving unselfishly, and worshipping unceasingly. I believe its time for a fresh manifestation of life and liberty in the church which will draw a spiritually hungry world into the joy of a living relationship with a living God.

The line is drawn: Either we continue to put up with the stale bread of dead religion, or we move forward into the full liberty of Christ. I, for one, choose freedom!

Conclusion

Some of you don't like this book. It scares you. We have pulled the rug out from under some old familiar furniture, and now the place is a mess. Maybe it's time for an update anyway. Maybe the Law was just supposed to be a tutor, a schoolmaster to lead us to Christ. (Galatians 3:24) It's possible, you know, that Christianity is not supposed to be about Law and rule-keeping anyway. Perhaps God was serious when He said He would dwell within us and guide us by His Spirit. What if His Spirit really is the teacher who guides us into all truth? (John 16:13) Perhaps, though it's a radical thought, to the pure all things really are pure. (Titus 2:15) Maybe the condition and intention of the heart is what really mattered to Him all along, anyway. (1 Samuel 16:7; 1 Corinthians 4:5)

For some of you, I may have raised more questions than I've provided answers. "What about pornography or internet porn," someone says, "Haven't you opened the door to rationalize filth?" Perhaps a door has been opened. I pray that it's not a door of compromise, but one of freedom. Now, however, it's time to become more discerning and self controlled. What is appropriate to view; what is inappropriate?

Now we have to face the burden of freedom. We are forced to wrestle with God and work out our own salvation with fear and trembling. (Philippians 2:12) What we end up working out may vary from person to person depending on several factors.

Our Kindergarten teachers were right when they taught us that each person, like the snowflake, is completely unique. Rules are not always absolute. What God allows in one instance, He prohibits in another. Each Spirit- indwelt believer now has a responsibility to follow the specific leading of God in each unique situation and circumstance. We are also called to submit our lives to godly authority that God will use to bring both confirmation and clarity.

In a sense, mere formula-based religion is easier to figure out than real relationship with God. Follow a few simple rules and you're ok; break a few commandments and you're out of here! Relationship, on the other hand, is a whole different thing altogether. God wants to speak; we desperately need to hear. He wants to lead, we desperately need to follow. Each destiny is different, each path unique.

As Christians we carry the intense, powerful light and life of God within us. It must be exposed to the darkness and allowed to shine forth into dark places. It's stronger than the darkness, and will ultimately overcome it.

I believe Christians can and must "occupy (new territory) until He comes." (Luke 19:13 KJV) This is not a time to think escape, but a time to overcome in Jesus Name! We're called to impact the world, not retreat from it.

Our light is indeed stronger than their darkness. Our love is stronger than their hatred. Our faithfulness is stronger than their failures. This is not to say we are perfect or have arrived. But we do believe, as Christians, that the perfect One lives inside us and He is continuously transforming us into the image of Christ. (2 Corinthians 3:18)

May God help us to become less judgmental and more

focused on what really matters. People don't need moral lectures, they need spiritual transformation. The world doesn't need us constantly boycotting, picketing, and cursing them; they need us to turn on the light and demonstrate God's glorious Kingdom through the way that we live and love. All men are supposed to know us by our love, not by our religious lingo, strange dress, or quirky ways. We are to touch the "lepers," not run away for fear of being contaminated.

What the world needs now is love, sweet love.

What the body of Christ needs is maturity, freedom and self-control.

What God desperately desires is someone to work with: Someone (or ones) that will look like Jesus; laugh like Jesus; transform the room like Jesus; light up the world like Jesus; offer hope and healing like Jesus; attract children like Jesus; relate to sinners like Jesus; build people up like Jesus; despise dead religion like Jesus; confront rigid traditions like Jesus; cast out demons like Jesus; teach with authority and life like Jesus, and most importantly of all – love like Jesus! May there be a new wave of incarnation - God becoming flesh and touching the world through the body of Christ. May we represent Him well, dwelling in the midst of a hurting world that so desperately needs to see His glory, experience His love, and be reconciled in relationship to Him.

"In the last days the mountain of the Lord's temple will be established as chief among the mountains; it will be raised above the hills, and all nations will stream to it. Many peoples will come and say, 'Come let us go up to the mountain of the Lord...He will teach us his ways, so that we may walk in his paths'...He will judge between the nations and will settle disputes for many peoples. They will beat their swords into plowshares and their spears into pruning hooks. Nation will not

take up sword against nation, nor will they train for war anymore. 'Come, O house of Jacob, let us walk in the light of the Lord'...Holy, holy, holy is the Lord Almighty; the whole earth is full of his glory... 'Woe to me!' I cried, 'I am ruined! For I am a man of unclean lips, and I live among a people of unclean lips'...he (one of the seraphs) touched my mouth and said, 'See, this has touched your lips; your guilt is taken away and your sin atoned for.' Then I heard the voice of the Lord saying, 'Whom shall I send? And who will go for us?' And I said, 'Here am I. Send me!" (Isaiah 2:1-5; 6:3-8)

Endnotes

[1] Aline Rousselle (translated by Felicia Pheasant) *Porneia* (New York, NY: Barnes & Noble Books, 1996), p.152.

[2] David Mace *A Christian Response to the Sexual Revolution* (Nashville, TN: Abingdon Press, reprint 1987) p. 55.

[3] Rousselle, p.152.

[4] Mace, p.56.

[5] James B. Nelson *Body Theology* (Louisville, KY: Westminster/John Knox Press, 1992), p.37.

[6] Mace, p. 135.

[7] Matthew Fox *Signs of the Spirit, Blessings of the Flesh* (New York, NY: Three Rivers Press, 1999), p.29.

[8] St. Augustine, *De Trinitate*, 7.7.

[9] Dwight Hervey Small *Christian: Celebrate Your Sexuality* (Old Tappan, New Jersey: Fleming H. Revel Co., 1974), p.58.

[10] Small, p.58.

[11] Michael Lamb "Hormones vs. Culture" *Psychology Today* (New York, NY) April 2002 edition.

[12] Nashville *Tennessean* (Nashville, TN: March 17, 2002).

[13] Lewis B. Smedes *Sex for Christians* (Grand Rapids, MI: Wm B. Eerdmans Publishing Co., 1976), p. 210.

[14]Ibid.

[15]Cecil Hook *Free to Change* (New Braunfels, TX: Cecil Hook, 1990), pp.74-75.

Also: Gareth Moore *The Body in Context* (London, England: SCM Press Ltd., 1992), p.14.

[16] Will Deming "A First Century Discussion of Male Sexuality" *New Testament Studies* (Oxford, UK: Studiorium, 1990) pp. 130-141.

[17]Spiros Zodhiates "Lexical Aids to the New Testament" *The Complete Word Study New Testament* (Chattanooga, TN: AMG Publishers, 1991), p.914.

[18] Ibid.

[19] Craig Blomberg *The New American Commentary Vol. 22* (Nashville, TN: Broadman Press, 1992), p. 109.

[20] Deming, pp.130-141.

[21] Moore, p.16.

[22] Blomberg, p.109.

[23] Robert and Mollie Brow *Adultery: An Exploration of Love and Marriage* (**www.brow.on.ca./Books/Adultery**), chapt. 6, pp.1-2.

[24] Zodiates, "Strong's Greek Dictionary of the New Testament" *The Complete Word Study New Testament*, Strongs NT, p.43.

[25]Gerhard Kittel (trans. by Geoffrey Bromiley) *TDNT Vol. 3* (Grand Rapids, MI: Wm B. Eerdmans Publishing Co., 1976), p.896.

[26] John Temple Bristow *What Paul Really Said About Women* (San Francisco, CA: HarperCollins Publishing, 1991), p.89.

[27] William Barclay *The Letters to Timothy, Titus, and Philemon* (Philadelphia, PA: The Westminster Press, 1975), p.67.

[28] Ibid.

Also Brian S. Rosner "Temple Prostitution in 1 Corinthains 6:12-20" *Novum Testamentum XL, 4* (Boston, MA: Brill Publishers, 1998).

[29] Paul Tillich Morality and Beyond (Louisville, KY: First Westminster John Knox Press, 1995 (reprint), p.66.

[30] Zodiates, Strong's #1261, p.22.

[31]Richard J. Foster "Sexuality and Singlenss" *Readings in Christian Ethics*

(Grand Rapids, MI: Baker Books, 1996), p.160.

32 Smedes, p.211.

33 Brow, Appendix F, p.2.

34 Foster, p.161.

35 Archibald D. Hart *The Sexual Man* (Dallas, TX: Word Publishing, 1994), p.136.

36 Small, pp.75-76.

37 Ibid, p.79.

38 John Duffy "Clitoridectomy: A Nineteenth Century Answer to Masturbation" (Presented at *The First International Symposium on Circumcision*, Anaheim, CA, March 1989), p.2.

39 "Review of European Legislation for Control of Prostitution" (editorial: *New Orleans Medical Journal*, 1854-55) 11: 700-705.

40 Duffy, p.1.

41 Ibid, p.3.

42 Vern L. Bullough "Technologies for the Prevention of 'Les Maladies Produites per la Masturbation Technology and Culture" (*The International Quarterly of the Society for the History of Technology*) 28:4, pp. 828-832.

43 Ellen E. Perkins "Sexual Armor" United States Government Patent #875,845. (Patented in 1908 – www.uwpto.gov), p.1.

44 Nelson, p.34.

45 Nelson, p.34.

46 "Self Love and Cereal II..." *History House* (www.historyhouse.com: 1996-2000), p. 2.

47 Charlie Shedd *The Stork is Dead* (W Publishing Group, reprinted 1983).

48 Spiros Zodiates The Complete Word Study Dictionary (Chattanooga, TN: AMG Publishers, 1992) p. 1339.

49 Tillich, p.66.

50 Tillich, p.69.

About the Author

Brad Watson is an evangelical, full-gospel minister who leads Harvest International Ministries (H.I.M.), an international, interdenominational, and multi-cultural network of ministers and ministries based out of Nashville, Tennessee, USA.
Known as an effective Bible teacher and communicator, Pastor Watson has a passion for igniting revival fires and challenging Christians to embrace the Kingdom priorities of Jesus Christ in a powerful, non-compromising, but culturally-relevant way.
His primary desire is to be a good husband, father, and mentor to his physical and spiritual family. Alongside him in life and ministry are his wife, Pastor Sheila; and daughters: Rachel, Sarah, and Anna Grace.

Contact Information:
Harvest International Church
www.harvestchristian.com
Rev. Brad Watson
PO Box 328
Hermitage, TN USA 37076
(615) 316-0085

Printed in the United States
61162LVS00002B/28-33